MADRE

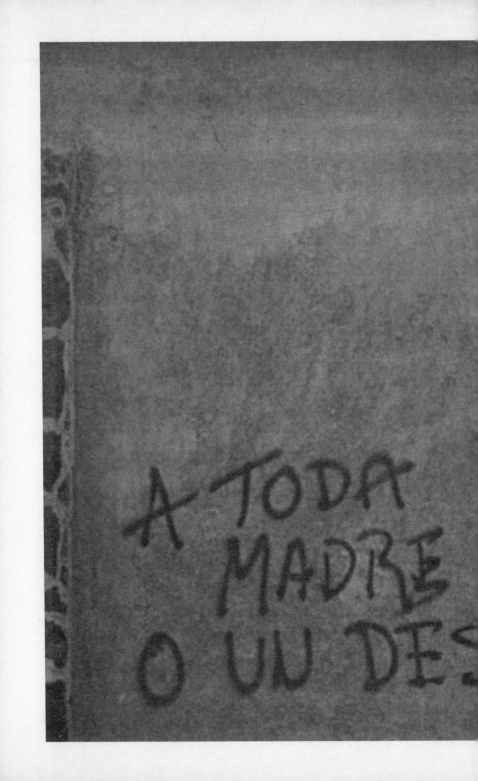

MADRE

PERILOUS JOURNEYS
WITH A
SPANISH NOUN

LIZA BAKEWELL

W. W. NORTON & COMPANY
New York   London

For information about permission to reproduce selections from this book,
write to Permissions, W. W. Norton & Company, Inc.,
500 Fifth Avenue, New York, NY 10110

For information about special discounts for bulk purchases, please contact
W. W. Norton Special Sales at specialsales@wwnorton.com or 800-233-4830

Manufacturing by Courier Westford
Book design by JAMdesign
Production managers: Andrew Marasia and Julia Druskin

Library of Congress Cataloging-in-Publication Data

Bakewell, Elizabeth.
Madre : perilous journeys with a Spanish noun / Liza Bakewell. — 1st ed.
p. cm.
Includes bibliographical references and index.
ISBN 978-0-393-07642-4
1. Spanish language—Noun. 2. Spanish language—Syntax. I. Title.
PC4201.B35 2010
465'.54—dc22

2010025494

W. W. Norton & Company, Inc.
500 Fifth Avenue, New York, N.Y. 10110
www.wwnorton.com

W. W. Norton & Company Ltd.
Castle House, 75/76 Wells Street, London W1T 3QT

1 2 3 4 5 6 7 8 9 0

To my parents

Thomas Woodhouse Bakewell and

Polly Oakleaf Bakewell

and my jewels

Jennie and Avery Bakewell

———————

CONTENTS

———

MADRE

INTRODUCTION

———

$\mathbb{F}$EBRUARY 23, 1987. Before I met Armando for dinner, I hailed a cab. I told the driver to head south on Insurgentes, right on La Paz, up over Revolución and into San Angel, then onto Juárez, later Hidalgo, and from there I directed him street by street. Right here, left there.

We turned onto a side street and into a neighborhood of salty white and sandy brown homes with lawns trimmed and polished as fine as I imagined the proprietors themselves. High adobe walls bordered these green oases. Wrought iron gates opened on occasion to let their owners in and out, as well as visitors and the occasional glance of a passerby. The neighborhood was interspersed with garbage-collecting empty lots, whose crumbling earthen walls struggled to maintain their separation from the street. On one of these someone had sprayed black paint, freehand, into large, unstylized letters, *A toda madre o un desmadre* floating it over the parched, craggy surface the way graffiti does everywhere in the world. Only this was legible.

"A total mother or a dis-mother" I tried to decipher it.

I had already heard, in the short time I had been in Mexico City, some extraordinary expressions with *madre* in them. *Me vale madre* was one of them.

What did it mean? The literal translation, "it is worth a mother," meant nothing to me.

"Worthless," someone told me.

"Worthless?" I asked, perplexed.

"Yes," someone else reiterated. As several others explained to me, the expression can be applied to just about anything— relationships, the government's rhetoric, the economy, the rise in random violence, dinner last night, the movie I wasted my pesos seeing.

I had never heard the expression in the Spanish classes of my college days. But when I first heard it shortly after arriving in Mexico, I held it in my hand as I might have held a strange insect. I studied it. I sought to locate it in a field guide to idiomatic Spanish insects, to no avail. Then someone translated it for me from one kind of Spanish to another kind of Spanish, from the literal "it's worth a mother," to the alley "it's worthless" or "I don't give a damn." I was even more baffled.

Also, around this time, I was introduced to its counterpart, the expression ¡Qué padre! Literally it translates as "what a father" and is said with exclamation, but figuratively it means, "How utterly fabulous, marvelous, amazing, and awesome."

"*Madre* is worthless and *padre* is marvelous?" I asked around.

"Yes," friends and acquaintances responded, followed by, "Well, más o menos." More or less.

And so began my journey with *madre*.

I HAD STARTED the first day of my journey as any other. I opened the curtains that ran the full length of the living room on a side street of what many claim to be the largest city in the world. At night they concealed a solid glass wall with a door at its far end. The door opened onto a narrow balcony where six potted hibiscus plants, each my height, a little over five feet tall, hovered together near the railing. Off to the right were two folding chairs, a small, painted metal table between them, and beyond that enough room for a person to stand and look out.

On this morning, as almost every day on the high valley plains of Mexico City, the sun burst in like a warm, bright blanket tossed in my direction. It felt like cashmere as it wrapped around me. I gripped my cup of instant coffee to warm my hands, which the night within the concrete walls of my apartment had dampened and made stiff, and I stood looking out onto the locomotion below me. My neighborhood had already unlocked its eyes, stretched right and left, arisen. It had sipped its coffee and hot chocolate, taken its buses, begun to drive its cars, walked its streets, and was lined up at kiosks to buy the daily papers, then off to work. It was always ahead of me in starting the day.

I pulled open the glass door and stepped out. Down on the street poor men accepted a few coins for washing and watching over parked cars as their commuting owners sauntered off to their appointments. Flower vendors filled their buckets with water on curbsides and intersections. Shop owners clanked open the heavy metal shades locked shut the night before at closing time. Men in orange overalls swept the streets with brooms made of brush.

From the second-story terrace, I felt a part of everyone's day, but also apart from it. I had moved here only a few weeks earlier from another neighborhood in the city and had begun to learn its geography, memorize its streets, the one where the outdoor market was located, the two that crossed on either side of the metro, the one whose blue wall contained a nook where a *taquería*—a restaurant dedicated to making and serving tacos—was tucked, the side alley where the nearest cobbler worked. I stayed here for two years. I lived here. It became my home, although I never fully fit in.

There were, on occasion, other pairs of blue eyes that I passed on the streets, and other blondes. But the combination of blonde and blue-eyed made me stick out, not to mention my New England, graduate-student look of high necklines and nontailored, loose-fitting clothes. And then there was my accent. I was an advertisement for an outsider, which is why I lapsed into thinking, from time to time while living here, how I had to start rolling my r's more, buy a pair of very high heels, stop wearing black, paint my fingernails (and, also, grow them), drop my neckline, and do something with my hair—other than tie it behind my head with the rubber band that held together yesterday's newspaper.

Also, I needed to stop looking so puzzled.

While I had read Spanish literature in college, this was the first time that I was surrounded by the sounds of Spanish and speaking it full time. It raised questions for me. Most of all, the word *madre*.

I couldn't stop asking, why, if one has any manners at all in Spanish-speaking Mexico, can't one say the word *madre*, the word for mother, without raising eyebrows or sometimes dodging punches?

How has it come to be that *madre* means whore as much as virgin and that you should give the word up altogether and talk, if you must, about one's *mamá*?

What happens to the ninety-nine Spanish-speaking madres seated in the auditorium after the one father enters and the Spanish feminine plural, *madres*, is cast aside for the male plural, *padres*, to describe the group of women plus one man? Do the madres cease to exist or are they there as before? Or are they there, but not as before, sequestered somewhere?

How is it that the Spanish word childbirth, *el parto*, is in the masculine, not to mention *el* love, *el* marriage, *el* sex, *el* pregnancy, and *el* birth, whatever the order, but death, *la muerte,* and life, *la vida*, are feminine?

And how can it be that some idiomatic expressions, like *me vale madre*, make absolutely no sense when translated, even when translated by a native speaker?

"It's worthless? How is that possible?" I would ask.

The honking of horns wrenched me from my thoughts, and after a few minutes in the sun, I walked back inside to read the morning papers, before I left to catch the cab.

From inside I could hear the ringing of a handheld bell sounding a C-flat. I envisioned the young man walking down the street
shaking it above his head. I had seen him many times before. His
job was to signal the arrival of the garbage truck that was only a
few minutes behind him. I heard the footsteps of housekeepers rush
from the building to the street with last night's waste, tied shut
with the plastic handles of supermarket bags. I had accompanied
them in this ritual many times, learning to hand the *basurero* my
trash and return upstairs in silence with everyone else. Soon the
sharp call of a man who bought used clothing pierced the air, then
the panpipes of the knife sharpener on bicycle, the hot-air whistle
of the *camote* vendor's steam pipe, his roasted potatoes creamy and
sweet. The scent of fresh tortillas. More sounds and smells wafted
my way, followed by the heat of the morning traffic.

Within the outpouring of urban motion, I drank my coffee
and read.

Time passed.

AT SOME POINT I thought to check the hour. I was about to be
late, because here in Mexico City one circumnavigates to a desti-
nation. The roads radiate rather than crisscross. Intersections are
trapezoidal and filled with oblique angles, others circular, like the
stagecoach roundabouts of Boston, only grander with Aztec emperors looking proud and triumphant in their centers or, in others, an
Angel of Independence, covered in gold, lighting atop a tall, stone
column. Away from the geometry of trapezoids and circles and into
the old residential neighborhoods, where I was headed, the roads
meander into a desultory mass of paved rivulets and unpaved, winding streams of dry, dusty earth. During the day the traffic is a long,
lazy caterpillar moving so slowly vendors come to the highways to
sell typewriters, hat stands, books, newspapers, and chewing gum.
Only during Catholic holidays, when most people who own cars
go on vacation, are the streets completely clear of traffic.

To make up for time, I first took the subway south to Barranca del Muerto (Dead Person's Ravine), the last stop on the Orange Line, the entrance of which was located only two short blocks from my apartment, and the last stop of which, the story goes, was named after a young boy found murdered there a century or so earlier. At Barranca del Muerto I hailed the cab.

The cab ride began with the driver easing into the wide, eight-lane boulevard of Revolución. We passed a few of the mansions scattered along its broad sides that were built a hundred years ago as summer homes for the wealthy who lived in the center of town. Each one had long ago fallen into disrepair and been engulfed by a horde of small stores and apartment buildings, by food vendors who each morning set up their kitchens for the day in front of them, and by masses of cars and buses that sped by them, oblivious to their former grandeur and the awe they once inspired.

We passed an occasional sixteenth-century church built with the stones of dismantled Aztec pyramids, eighteenth-century plazas with shaded arcades wrapped around them as protection from the afternoon heat and rains, multistoried, twentieth-century construction sites of glass and concrete with workers standing on the edge of steel beams.

We passed an electric blue, six-foot-tall condom with boxing gloves, beating the HIV retrovirus into submission. Alive and in living color, it was on a billboard that stood between two cement buildings, a sensibility so foreign to any found in New England, where I lived when I wasn't here, it made me smile. It was anathema to the Vatican, however, and so a few weeks before the Pope came to Mexico City in the early 1990s, these billboards were dismantled. Because abstinence, dear people, is God's Way. Millions and millions in Mexico, the country with more baptized Roman Catholics than any other country in the world outside Brazil, stopped what they were doing to attend large outdoor masses and hear the Holy See. While the 1917 Constitution limited Church power, much like its predecessor, the Constitution of 1857, written by anti-Church Liberals, President Salinas (1988–1994) wanted to reverse all that a bit. So, he did. Maybe because he had not received a mandate from the people in the presidential elections, just barely squeaking in. He invited the Pope to Mexico, restored diplomatic relations with the Vatican, and changed articles of the Mexican Constitution to make that all possible. But those decisions took a toll on some billboards.

We passed a thousand more pedestrians. At red lights we inhaled the smells of hot corn *masa*, tacos, tamales, quesadillas, onions, and cilantro that women and men cooked on fire-hot, terracotta *comales*, outdoors on sidewalk corners.

The driver asked if I had children.

And when I said no, he continued.

"Oh, you and your husband can't have children?"

Of the 300 taxis I took in the city, 290 of their drivers asked me these questions.

I looked out the window at the traffic and thought nostalgically of Catholic holidays, not only for the opened boulevards, but also for how, without the cars, the air resumes its famed transparency. I thought how the volcanoes resurface at the edge of the valley like gods, towering above the clouds, 17,000 feet above sea level and snowcapped; how ancient, majestic, and formidable they are. It is during these smogless days that the gray of the city's concrete, which overshadowed the days here, lifts like fog. And history reappears, like the day Cortés rode over the volcanic mountain pass and saw for the first time this magnificent valley, filled with water.

It was at this point in the cab ride that I saw the madre graffiti. I opened my notebook and jotted it down.

"And you. Do you have children?" I asked the driver in return, while unable this day to see the plume issue forth from Popocatepetl's cone, the tallest of the two volcanoes closest to the city, the upright and masculine Popo next to the supine Ixtaccihuatl, as the folklore appears in *taquería* calendar art.

"Yes. I have three."

And he told me about each one. The oldest who was attending college, another on her way to college, a third living in Chicago with an uncle. He did not mention his children's mother. No taxi driver ever did mention her.

I paid him the fare, wished his family well, and rang the bell at the gate of the house, where I conducted one of two prearranged interviews.

But as I went through my day tape-recording conversations with artists, who graciously responded to my countless questions, there in the back of my mind was the graffiti I had seen from the taxi window, along with the other madres I had met previously, hovering like noisy helicopters in the mountainous terrain of befuddlement, looking for a place to land.

WHEN ARMANDO MET up with me in the late afternoon, I described my day to him. After he heard that the taxi driver had inquired about my having children, Armando gave me a what-planet-are-you-from look. "Taxi drivers want to know if you are available for a date or more," he said, and continued to roll his eyes. As did all my friends here, when I played back the day's events for them because to Armando and everyone else it was obvious. But to me, nothing ever is when it arrives in a foreign language, traveling over a foreign geography through foreign air and sunlight, bubbling up from foreign soil, where it had rested during a foreign night before.

While we were on the topic of appropriate behavior, I told him about a man I saw masturbating on my street in front of my apartment window, and looking straight up at me, it seemed, a few days earlier. Armando worried and said there are bad men, and there are good ones. He only knew the good ones, he assured me. The story of this "bad" man made him feel protective of me.

After I told him about the graffiti and asked him how to translate it, he was circumspect.

"Can you explain this expression to me?" I prodded.

"*A toda madre* is a fabulous situation. A *desmadre*, a disaster," he responded. Politely. And told me that they were not expressions I should use.

"Why? And what does madre have to do with it?"

But he wasn't sure. "They are just expressions. They have no literal meaning. No word-for-word translation," he said.

On the one hand, he was unsure because idioms are natural aspirations to a native, practically part of the autonomic nervous system, and like idioms everywhere their idiomatic wholes do not result from the sum of their parts.

On the other hand, he left it at that. Politeness and silence are good partners. Or is it *politics* and silence?

But these idioms were not without cargo, and I could see that he was thinking about them. Which is why I kept bothering him. I still bother him over the phone, two-and-then-some decades later. "How is it possible?" and "I don't get it, do you?" To this day he is still circumspect, having loosened up over the years only a wee bit.

That evening, as I lay awake in bed, I wondered how I would package the day into a list of reflections and insights, an exercise I sometimes did at night instead of counting sheep. I took out my notebook and wrote:

graffiti about mothers, total mothers and dis-mothers
condoms, alive, the size of a billboard and in living color
the volcano Ixtaccihuatl and her partner, Popocatepetl
Catholic holidays
the Pope
anticlerical Constitutions
tacos and tamales made and sold by men and women on street corners
construction sites
Aztec emperors and winged victories inside traffic circles
conversations with taxi drivers about children

a taciturn Armando
linguistically awesome fathers
other expressions with madre
all the madres I had yet to hear or see

Then, once my list was done, I placed a check next to "*graffiti about mothers, total mothers* and *dis-mothers*," thinking that in the morning I would set myself on the task of writing about it, attempt a translation and explanation for a couple of hours with my morning coffee.

Even back then I had a hunch that the entries I made that evening in my sleepy head were inextricably related to one another, like a ball of yarn after the cat had it. And so it turned into an impossible task to single out any one item for cross-examination without all the others coming along in a messy heap. This messy heap grew in size and texture and untidiness over the months and years ahead, as I continued to lay awake, recalling where I'd been, what I'd seen and heard each day while living in Mexico and visiting over the next two decades.

SOMETIME AFTER THE turn of the century, while I was still making lists, I set out to write a *short* book on the word *madre* in Mexico. I thought that if I could figure it out once and for all, I would be as close to a native speaker as anyone who grew up here. And it wouldn't require too much work, only one word, not the whole dictionary, not even a page of the dictionary. Just one word, with only two syllables and five basic letters. I'd taken notes for two decades. I had written a dissertation on Mexico. And I had taught linguistic anthropology to undergraduates as a graduate student and later when I became a professor.

The *short* part of the book plan was important because with two young toddlers, which is what I had when I started writing, and being the only one who was around to take care of them—while holding down a job that involved excessive grant writing, lots of creative energy, external deadlines, and travel—I wanted to be alive when I reached the conclusion.

But I ran into problems. It turns out that madre under intense scrutiny, like a cell under a microscope, is filled with more activity than I had planned and had seen with my own two eyes over the years. There are atoms inside this madre cell, filled with energy and whizzing around and around in elliptical swirls.

That is to say that language under a microscope can seduce a person into hours of detective work. One can zoom in on any one part or movement, follow a line of inquiry, take this detour and that, and never come back. I know of people who years ago put a phoneme, the smallest unit of meaningful sound, under a microscope and never stopped looking at it their whole careers. Their books are short, but their research hours long. There's a lot going on inside big *and* small parts of speech that can carry you off without your even knowing.

So what began as a harmless, late-night itemization, envisioned as a quotidian exercise of anthropological inquiry into the social life and culture of my day, became a multidisciplinary exploration of a two-syllable word that involved hundreds of friends and acquaintances, not to mention linguists, lexicographers, grammarians, philologists, philosophers, cognitive scientists, archaeologists, primatologists, historians, fellow anthropologists, and even biologists. So that at one point I had a metaphorical microscope out on my dining room table with the sound *m* on a glass slide, and I was chanting and humming and feeling vibrations while increasing the magnification.

Also, madre, like any other cell, has never lived alone. She's all tangled up with the outside, not only in Mexico with its complicated history, but with the Spanish language, going back to the conquistadors, Arabs and Arabic, Roman soldiers, spoken Latin, written Latin, Greek, other Indo-European languages, Proto-Indo-European roots, all of human prehistory, Africa, the human vocal tract, the earliest sounds ever made. Savannahs, trees, and primates. And who knows from there, maybe right on back to a grouping of single cells, fit, surviving, and multiplying.

And then there's the ongoing problem of finding these linguistic madres in the towns and cities of Mexico. I'd been looking for them for almost two decades before starting this book. But a number of unwritten codes keep them under wraps. Madre lives in a man's world; *cultured* women do not use these expressions, Armando had told me when we first met. In addition, grammatical rules like the masculine default bind them up, further. There are plenty of "good" madres that are right out there, and I'm thinking now about the Virgin Mother and all her incarnations and incantations in a place like Mexico, not to mention throughout Latin America and Spain. But I wanted to understand all the hidden ones. Hence, a bumpy journey, winding and, on occasion, precipitous.

I did not travel alone but with a motley cast of Spanish-speaking friends and acquaintances, all real people like Armando, although I have given a few of them new names at their request. They talk and question and have opinions about Spanish, while eating tacos and enchiladas and drinking tequila and *cerveza,* while looking at art in an artist's studio, shooting the breeze with a taxi driver, listening to a priest from the pews of a church, or pouring a bowl of cereal in a kitchen on the coast of Maine, far from Latin America, with a cup of Mexican, Colombian, or Costa Rican coffee, brought directly up from the farms and cities south of the border, to warm the homesick soul.

At times it may seem that we wander off the topic, but the tangents are all related. Language has a symbiotic relationship with us. We keep each other alive. Language helps us to communicate our love for someone or our anger with another. We use it to report on the day's happenings or remind each other of yesterday's events and future hopes and promises. We discuss our plans and map them out in outlines and lists. We imagine, narrate, denounce, implore. We weave ourselves and others into stories of romance and betrayal.

But there's more.

Language moves us. It causes us to feel included, excluded, loved, rejected, commemorated, meditative, forgotten. It can make us feel bigger or smaller than we actually are. It does this quietly, drawing very little attention to itself. Most of us think it's the speakers' doings, and we give them all the credit or hand over all the blame. We don't even notice what language is up to, so much of the time. But words as much as speakers are doing the doing.

JUST THE OTHER day I stopped traveling with madre. Because after twenty-three years since that fateful cab ride, my list of notes stretched out of my office window and for miles down the road. The neighbors banded together, *It is time for you to stop.* That's when I printed my most up-to-date thoughts on her, or what I now call "my two-syllable handful," folded them back and forth like a Mesoamerican codex, sliced their folds, placed covers at either end, and wrote nothing more than *madre* on its cover. I called Armando one more time. After that I checked in with a few other friends and acquaintances.

Then I said "et cetera" three times, with excessive drama.

That helped.

But like young children placed between covers, each night when asked to fall asleep, there was a split second of motionlessness. And then, when I turned my back, everything started to move again.

That's the nature of the word *madre.*

I mean *motion.*

It's not so easy to translate.

WEDDING

A S IT turns out, Armando could have translated the graffiti
A toda madre o un desmadre this way: "fabulous or a fuckup."

"But Armando, I don't understand," I announced from the passenger seat of his silver Chevy Impala, when I told him the translation others had whispered in my ear after I had seen the madre
graffiti.

We were on our way to a wedding, although we were dressed
in black because in Mexico, as Armando informed me in the nick
of time, one wears black to evening weddings.

"Black?" I thought of funerals as I grabbed a dark dress from
my closet.

"It's elegant."

It was late afternoon on Saturday. Like the calm after the windy
whitecaps of Friday rush hour, the city streets were still. Not the
stillness they have during a Catholic holiday, but close. Rippled
only for a moment by Armando passing through.

He was a good driver. I can't say that about all the drivers I met,
but like them, he was fast, which is why he avoided rush hour.
Also, for him, Mexico's love of one-way streets was a nuisance.
Not to mention its love of *topes* or traffic bumps that the Mexican
authorities impose on drivers, rather than take any chances with

setting speed limits. It's a different approach from what you have up north. More like a physical blow versus a legal request. The first one always works, however. The second one, más o menos. But the stop-and-go's of the first are extreme in Mexico. Whiplash-ing. I can't think of any other word to describe their relationship to the passenger in Armando's car.

Armando especially loved to drive around the city when he could cruise its streets with abandon. He would take questionable shortcuts, disregard lane divisions, not bother with signals, and then drive up onto sidewalks and around the topes.

"But Armando, it's one way. And *not* this way!" I exclaimed on our way to the wedding. Zipping his car up a one-way street the wrong way was his idea of efficiency, a relief from the morass of unidirectional side streets that composed my neighborhood.

"It's okay," he said at full speed. "It's Saturday. There's hardly anyone around." Other times he'd say, "Don't worry. It's Sunday." Or Easter or the Virgin's birthday.

I'm not Catholic. And by the time I was speeding down Mexico's side streets with Armando, I had outgrown my love of breaking the law, not to mention roller coasters. But it was times like these that I thought of converting to one side or the other instead of hanging within the secular straight and narrow. There were no air bags in those days. So I prayed like crazy for the Virgin, Christ, God, and the Holy Spirit to look over me, a rosary at the very least to grip instead of the dashboard, when weekends and holidays came around and I was whirling about town with Armando. For distraction I found temporary solace inside the cushions of conversation topics that required out-of-body contemplation. Mexican slang was always a good one.

"Armando. How is it that *a toda madre* and *desmadre* translate the way they do?" I tried to make the question feel new. "Can you connect the dots for me, throw me a line, build me a bridge? Can you help ferry me over to the other side, transfer me with some clues?"

Silence.

"And, also, by the way, why mother and not father?"

Not a peep.

So I filled the void. I mentioned that a few days ago I had heard *de poca madre,* another expression with mother in it. Literally "of little mother."

"It means 'great,'" someone had told me.

"Great? You've got to be kidding." Sure enough I realized the way it means great. It goes like this, unique, singular, happened all by itself, with little if any maternal intervention. Therefore, "great."

"Armando, do I have that right?"

He nodded.

A response. We're getting somewhere, I thought.

And so I added *de poca madre* to my list, along with *a toda madre, un desmadre, me vale madre,* which I translated in this way: great for being absent; great for being present in some form or other; a fuckup; and worthless or I don't give a damn. Soon enough a pattern started to take shape.

"Wait a minute. A toda madre, a lot of mother, and de poca madre, from a little mother, both mean the same thing?" The pattern was topsy-turvy.

"Yes. In a way they do."

"How is that? In what way?"

"I don't know," and he switched the topic.

THE STUDY OF language can occur just about anywhere. But if carried out by a linguistic anthropologist, it usually occurs in situ, rather than out-of-situ, on a street rather than in a lab. Villages and urban neighborhoods are perfect for the anthropology of language; kitchens with a lot of cooks can be gold mines; taxis and bars with strangers offer treasure chests; Armando's car, with only Armando and me, turned out to be chock full of goodies, once I understood a few things about it. Because in the *performance* of language—when stories are told, conversations evolve, gestures and intonations are made—a *no* accompanied by a silent wink might mean *yes*, but you'd have to be there to know. And you have to be there to see everything else: Was it a woman or a man speaking and to whom; from what class; what cohort; what time of day, month, year; when in history; in the kitchen or the bar; what was everyone wearing? The anthropologist's approach revels in the fluidity of language, its infinite variations, its heterogeneity, the way speakers and listeners manipulate their communication, the way the variables of gender, class, region, age, education, ritual, religion, and the like interact with what's said and how it is understood within these performances. And then there's pure play, rhythm and rhyme, tone and style, twisted grammar and far-flung punctuation.

The problem for me has always been, where and at what point do I draw the line? Which is why on occasion all I wanted was a direct, well-defined answer from anyone here in Mexico about anything at all concerning madre. Early on in this journey, I hadn't planned to write a book on the word. Back then I had only wanted to understand Spanish and Mexico better so I could carry on like a native.

Armando cleared his throat.

Well, okay, like a native . . . bricklayer.

"So, what *does* this or that madre mean?"

Nada.

"Armando, are you there?"

But he remained quiet on the topic.

"Because Armando, aren't mothers worshipped here, your mother, that guy's mother?" I asked him frequently. This time I mentioned the Mexican painter Magali Lara who had waxed eloquent on the topic with me. Warm houses, kitchens, food, and savory smells came to her mind, when she thought of Mexican mothers. I reminded him of all the wonderful stories he had told me of his mother.

"Yes," he interrupted, "but not *that guy's* mother," and laughed, while taking his hands off the wheel to smooth the lapels of his suit.

Was he nervous?

I was petrified.

"And what about the entire country's love of the Virgin Mother, the Virgin Mary, and the Virgin of Guadalupe?" I continued. There is no person alive in Mexico who can't go on and on about the Virgin of Guadalupe—non-Catholics included. She's not just a religious figure, she's a cultural icon. She's at the very heart of national identity. After she appeared to a hardworking indigenous man, Juan Diego, in the sixteenth century, the story goes, she consecrated the ground under her, legitimized Spain's presence in the hemisphere, and later justified the War of Independence from Spain. Later the state draped Mexican flags over her image in many churches, claiming her as its Protector. Mexico was a chosen land. There are Mexicans who claim with great pride, I am *guadalupana* or *guadalupano*, in the masculine if a man, meaning they are believers in *Her*, and that makes them *really* Mexican, ones living in the aura of her Grace.

In the four months I had been in Mexico, I had already seen at least a million representations of the Virgin of Guadalupe. In months to come I'd see another million. Armando had pointed out to me the Colonial ones inside church altars and tucked into courtyards off beaten paths. But on my own and with other friends I had seen her painted into murals and onto canvases and scraps of tin, molded into statues of clay and plastic, placed on bedside tables, street corner shrines, and dashboard altars. There was the ceramic one nestled in the outer southwest corner of the red house on the way to a friend's in Tizapán. Another covered with plastic flowers at the bus stop behind the market. The enshrined one in front of the small church in the plaza across the street. The one at the taxi stand on Magdalena. Another next to the spark plug posters in the back of shops where shoes are cobbled, business cards printed, suits tailored, and where afternoon chats percolate in the interstices of the day. All the Virgins inside private chapels, homes, subways, *peseros*, *combis*, buses, and cars. The ones cascading down plunging necklines. The miniature one inside the shoe shiner's wooden box, the size of his ring finger.

"This is the land of mother worship," I exclaimed.

"Yes. Yes."

"So why are these idioms, at least in my notebook, beginning to add up to a list of mixed signals, that is, praise mixed with disdain?"

Just then he saw something out the corner of his eye, a beautiful church, a delicious restaurant, a friend's home, and with these sights his ticket to change the topic. Because, as it continued to turn out, madre was not a word that a Mexican gentleman would use, or analyze for that matter, in front of a lady. It wasn't polite. Also, it wasn't politic. And Armando was *bién* educated, not to mention a politician of sorts.

The truth is that it was hard to get a straight answer from Armando on anything at all, much less mothers. His indirectness in most areas was not a problem, we usually arrived at the punch line one way or another, but when it came to linguistic madres, it had an impact on just how border-crossing a speaker he was going to let me become.

"Armando, I'm an anthropologist," I sometimes pleaded with him.

But no go. At least no direct go. As faithful a friend as he was, when it came to helping me out with my inappropriate Spanish, his approach was the linguistic analog to the circumnavigations of ground travel here—roundabout.

In retrospect I see that Armando's circumlocutions turned me into a linguistic anthropologist, when before I was perfectly happy being a cultural anthropologist with a side interest in language. Both his silences and subject-turnings drove my curiosity beyond where I had wanted to go. They gave me a craving, like the ones that overcome me for dessert the moment I put myself on a diet. I was driven.

At some point, though, I saw that his roundabouts and his silences weren't empty at all but filled with clues. Take the wedding we attended in the spring of 1987. It gave me what I needed to make connections from madre to the world of marriage rituals and church iconography, Catholic narratives of human sexuality, and definitions of motherhood. That was critical. And from his silences I learned that it was improper for a woman to say *madre* but not for a man. He was letting me know that madre moved around in a man's world. There was meaning in that. Public definitions of motherhood have been constructed by men for eons. Why wouldn't that be true here, as well, for the Spanish word *madre*? Yes, of course.

I MET ARMANDO before I met almost anyone else in Mexico. He was the unemployed brother of an art historian I hoped to meet someday. As it turned out, after kissing the air next to my cheek, Armando felt the same way toward me as I would later feel toward Mexicans visiting the United States, sympathetic, because I was out of context and needing help with my To Do list.

I had come to Mexico City to conduct fieldwork on the relationship of politics to art for a doctorate in anthropology, and to accomplish that I needed to attend a number of functions that occurred at night. Armando started to look for me in the early evening because, he asserted, it would be dangerous for me to do anything of the sort at those hours without an escort. Not because he feared I might be the victim of a crime. In the late 1980s the crime rate in Mexico City was relatively normal for a megalopolis. But because he was chivalrous. I was a young, single woman and alone. And had I been among a group of women, I would still have been alone because without a man, that's how the situation is perceived here. And thank God for Armando's good manly manners, because I have always been afraid of the dark, which complicated going to nighttime gallery openings, round table discussions, book signings, theater, and the like. So while he remained unemployed, he became my evening accomplice.

Armando had lost his government job shortly after the change of Mexican presidents. The *sexenio* turnover every six years is routine, not to mention the law. But it's a tidal wave in the chaos it produces for many of its workers, and the number of swimmers it tosses and turns. While many people caught up in this situation are quickly recycled from one position to another, in and out of government, Armando was not. He remained unemployed for years. So as time went on he became my daytime co-conspirator, as well. We went everywhere together, even on vacations.

In return I helped Armando forget he was unemployed.

As it turned out, Armando's etiquette drove only part of his evasiveness. There were several reasons that impelled him to skirt the madre issue and other issues he wanted to avoid. For example, his love of the subjunctive. In English the subjunctive form of a verb, described in grammar books as a "mood" rather than a "tense," plays a minor role, more a part of its archaeology than its living organism. The little that is left continues to fight the tides of the indicative and the declarative. "Verb tenses tell *when* something happens; moods tell *how true*," wrote Michele Morano, while living in Spain.[1] We say in English, with a glimmer of hope, "If it were only true." But we say it rarely. We prefer, "Tomorrow, when Joe arrives, we will eat" or "We hope he will bring Ellie with him," putting all verbs in the indicative, even when we can't know for a fact that these events will take place.

But in Spanish life's uncertainties and contingencies show up in the subjunctive, which is alive and well and bubbling all over in communities that speak it, so that the *arrives* of "when Joe arrives" and the *will bring* of "we hope he will bring" would occur in the subjunctive, as if translated into, "when Joe might arrive" and "we hope he might bring." And there are many, many other cases in which the subjunctive is deployed, for example, for expressing wishes, desires, happiness, sadness, anger, possibility, probability;

when something is good or important; when there is doubt and disbelief or hope and wishful thinking; when there are objectives; when there is time involved, as in "when Joe arrives," when the adverbial phrases—in case that, in order that, unless, before, provided that—are used; when the subordinating conjunctions—when, as soon as, until, after—are used; when one gives advice or recommendations to others. And, though this may sound oxymoronic to an English-language reader, the subjunctive is used in uttering a command. That is to say, the imperative and the subjunctive are grammatically configured the same. So that, the *go* of "Go to the store and buy us milk, please, before Joe arrives" (*Vaya a la tienda a comprarnos leche, por favor, antes de que llegue Joe*) is in the subjunctive as much as it is in the imperative.

While living in Mexico with the subjunctive all around me, I was often reminded of the word *ilusión*, which came to represent for me a visual analog of this mood. The Mexican artist Elena Climent introduced me to the word when I first heard her talk about her paintings, which at the time contained the odds and ends that make up people's lives here, the objects they have collected, the mementos from trips taken, the keepsakes stuffed into corners here and there. She called the still lifes she painted *rincones de ilusión*. That was not to be understood as "corners of illusion," she explained to me, intercepting any ill-fated translation I might unconsciously make, but "islands of optimism."

She was right to intercept. In English when I hear the word *illusion*, I immediately make a string of associations that go like this: unscientific, false, delusion, fantasy, chicanery, wrong, mistaken, deceptive, on drugs. But in Spanish, the word *ilusión* emphasizes the imaginative aspect of reality, while it contains in its meaning part of the nonreal of the English. An ilusión is suggestive, it attracts. An ilusión emphasizes the hopeful. It can mean a lively infatuation with a person, a thing, a task, or chore. The closest analogy I can make in my English-speaking world is with the Wizard of Oz, but not for his deception. While he was not, as we find out, a wizard at all, he did have a great and powerful humanistic ability to believe and to convince others to believe. For that he was not a fraud or an illusion, but a dispenser of ilusión.

Many times Spanish grammatically requires you to use the subjunctive. The *arrives* of "when Joe arrives" must be put into the subjunctive. But sometimes it's a speaker's choice. For example, you can put *enroll*, *eat*, and *kiss* into the subjunctive *or* the indicative when you say, "It is possible that I will enroll in that program," "Let's eat dinner out tonight," "Maybe later I'll kiss him." It depends on how much you believe it, how much hope or doubt or wonder you may have inside you at the moment you say it. It depends on the rincones de ilusión inside your collected outlook on life at that moment.

This hopeful, optimistic, doubtful, ambiguous, ambivalent, uncertain, very real mode of discourse was convenient for Armando because it helped him sidestep touchy topics that concerned pinning things down to who, what, when, where, and why. In my opinion he overused it. But declaring with the indicative gave him the shivers. So he'd answer my questions with a "maybe" or even a "probably" followed by verbal sub*junctiv*ity, but never a "It's certain that," followed by the indicative. While unsettling for me, it kept him clearing the hurdles.

Something else. I had to learn that Armando's "maybes" did not lean to either yes or no. They lingered unflappably inside limbo, like the souls of children who died before being baptized, still so full of temptation. When he at times used yes, I had to determine when his yes meant no. Or for that matter when his no meant yes. Even when the yes or no was exclaimed with an *absolutely*. Because it is more polite to say yes or maybe than it is to say and mean no. He wanted to keep my hopes up, but also he was in charge and didn't want me to know.

One more observation. He needed to be available in case something popped up. If he committed too early to doing something with me or to a thought or opinion he had about someone or something, he might miss an opportunity to have lunch or a drink with a person with an address book, a network, a line on a job opening. He was unemployed and wanted a job. I kept forgetting that.

So, instead of drawing upon the indicative and making declarative sentences, Armando took me sightseeing and out for tacos, using his savings to pay for the two of us, on occasion giving in to my insistence that I pay. Together we went for walks downtown, into churches built by local laborers and overseen by Spaniards four hundred years ago, to weddings, baptisms, birthdays, funerals, and cemeteries, when bands were singing and gravestones were being scrubbed of soot. He transported me up and down boulevards after rush hour. He wanted to educate me as much as possible about Mexican politics, art, architecture, rituals, foods, and language, so long as they were the highbrow kind. And Armando had a way with history. He was able to resuscitate it with just the right adjective or little-known fact. He knew not only where famous people had slept but with whom. On that last note alone, I began to think he was more an academic out of a job than a banker out of one. Or my grandmother reincarnated, whose fascination with French history overflowed with those very same details.

ON OUR WAY to the wedding Armando drove us out of the one-way streets of my neighborhood with the ease of a seasoned bandit and headed south down the open boulevards. From the car window I could see the old mansions again, and the newer buildings surrounding them. They were stately on these days— although, perhaps, lonely. Few vendors came around on weekends, and even fewer pedestrians. Only an occasional taxi or bus.

We turned onto a series of smaller streets where we passed a woman who was seated next to a large, steaming hot, restaurant-sized, heavy aluminum pot. A line of apron-clad women had formed off to her left, along the sidewalk. She was selling tamales, Armando told me. We were close to his neighborhood now. He mentioned the ones stuffed with chicken and hand molded with a spoonful of green chili, the others filled with strawberries, their cornmeal flesh sweetened and died pink with the red juice of the cooked berries.

"We'll pick some up tomorrow. You'll see how good they are." Then he laughed unselfconsciously, always jolly about the predictable impact such foods would have on his belt notch.

Not long after passing the *tamal* woman, we arrived at the Convent of Churubusco, where the wedding was about to take place. We were alive. Hallelujah. I considered it a miracle because we had flown so close to the ground, barely missing the wires, and Armando, as you have no doubt noticed, rarely looked at the road. From the exterior wall that encircled the convent where we joined the other early arrivals, I could see only a blue and white tiled chapel cupola with yellow majolica seams peering out from under the pruned canopy of a lacey treetop. Its shiny, low-fired glaze sent the long light of afternoon out to the rest of the universe in a misty rose halo. We stepped into the courtyard and stood under the celestial glow, while we waited in front of the closed church doors.

Armando had invited me to the wedding because he knew how much anthropologists love rituals. Rituals are the main reason many of us go into the business. For Armando the wedding was to be part of my graduate-school education, the one he directed, not that ivy-walled, secular one back in the States somewhere. Also, he didn't want to go alone. I helped deflect the question, When on earth are you ever going to have a *novia* and get married? Girlfriend, fiancée, and bride are all part of the same word in Spanish, so he had to be careful. You say "novia," and "I do" might come nipping at your heels in the mind of your interlocutor. "Never" was the answer he wanted to give, followed by "Would never ever be okay with you?" But he didn't dare in those days.

He was my age back then. I suppose he's still my age, but because he maintained his single, childfree life, he no doubt looks better than I do. I can only imagine because I haven't seen him for almost ten years, unless you count his pixelated appearances in the past year on my computer screen, thanks to our newly acquired built-in video cameras. At some point Armando found a job, and this put an end to our gallivanting about town together. Then, not long after landing the job, he was transferred to Europe where he has made a new home for himself. He no longer bothers to disguise his marital plans. Besides, in London, where he resides now, no one cares.

Armando lived with his parents like most unmarried Mexicans in the twentieth century. He also cared for them. He bought them their house. He took them to doctors' appointments. He carried their groceries. He drove them to see relatives in other parts of Mexico. In return his parents prayed for his well-being, and hoped that someday he would have a nice fiancée who would say to him, at the altar, "I do," and see to it that he led a healthy and happy adult life. There would be grandchildren.

When I met his parents, which was within days of knowing Armando, they had that look in their eyes of expectation. I was surely the one to marry their son. They called me *Linda Preciosa*, "Pretty Precious," which I took to be a crowning title like Queen, although in retrospect I was ambitious because it was more like an unaffiliated princess, as I came without many, if any, credentials, and my blonde hair had little to do with my bloodline. Either way, to them I was some kind of jewel in the crown of their son because I was with him, and he was their prince. Even when they discovered we were only friends, they never dropped my title. They asked me to sit and have a cup of coffee with them, which I did, but only on occasion, because sitting still was not what Armando liked to do, unless it was in a taquería. When we stopped to say hello to his parents or pick something up at his house, we were inevitably on our way out the door, just as we were walking through it.

ARMANDO ACCEPTED THE invitation to attend the wedding not because of any desire to go to church. His last whispered message to me before the ceremony began and as we watched the bride reach the groom at the altar, was that, while he loved the architectural and art history of churches, he avoided attending church services as much as possible. In all due respect to God, the Pope, and the Virgin of Guadalupe, Armando was Catholic but not that Catholic. All my upper-middle-class friends in Mexico had the same attitude. It was as though they knew they were getting away with something, the way a child giggles while stealing a cookie from the pantry in broad daylight and in front of a benevolent parent who, despite a scornful look, will inevitably commute the time-out sentence and be amused by the crime so long as respect for parental authority remains in check elsewhere. My upper-class and lower-middle-class friends didn't have the same sense of humor. They took the church more seriously. At the very least they believed in confession.

The truth is that Armando came to network. There is no greater social and professional networking opportunity than can be found at the wedding of a fancy family. I accompanied him like a dutiful politician's wife as he kissed every one of the guests, who were now swelling into a crowd outside the church. After each kiss he then turned to introduce me. I remember wondering, Does he know all 350 of them? Not that I stood there counting. I read the number in the social pages of the newspapers the next morning. They were mostly bankers. Many he had met during his school days. He acted as though he knew them, so I guess he did. Part of the confusion for me was that Mexicans don't shake hands so much as kiss the side of each other's cheeks. It doesn't mean any more than "Hello," but I come from a land where kisses, even the airborne kind, are not for acquaintances. We don't even dole out smiles much.

Armando fit into this well-heeled crowd with ease. If he was *mestizo*, which statistically the majority of Mexicans are, he was at the European end of the spectrum, without a visual hint of indigenous blood in him anywhere. This alone gave him class status in the city. His eyes were the color of the Spanish Mediterranean; his skin, more fawn than brown. His family tree had roots that ran, with no local detours, directly from their house in Mexico City to Iberia. Indeed, they had never been fully torn from the rich and rocky olive-growing soil of Spain in spite of living for numerous generations in the New World. That's what both his parents graciously maintained, and their living room furniture backed up the claim with its heavyset, upholstered Spanish chairs and thickly framed, colonial paintings of the life-sized Christ and Virgin Mother. They made me think of the Escorial, regal, solemn, and Old World, or of the Prado during Franco's time, before the galleries were repainted and relit after his death.

Armando's mother was as Catholic as a Spanish nun. She prayed regularly. She used only *usted*, the formal "you" and expected it to be used on her, keeping everyone's intimate second person *tu* at a respectful distance. This would have been normal in parts of the countryside, where using *usted* is so common that even spouses and siblings can be heard addressing each other with it. But in Mexico City, the more familiar *tu* is used among family and friends after a while, if not right away. She never dressed casually, and she transformed select Mexican consonants into Castilian *thetas*, making her even more Spanish than the Spaniards.

Armando was one of the shorter guests, however, as wealthy Mexicans can be tall. He was my height precisely, which made whispering gossip into my ear easy and instantaneous. Because I rarely wore heels, he would have remained my height had it not been for his classy education, which gave him extra stature. This was especially true of his business degree, which he earned from IPADE, the Instituto Panamericano de Alta Dirección de Empresa, a school owned by the Opus Dei, a conservative, lay Catholic organization that many people outside the Catholic church know from the albino monk, Silas, of *The DaVinci Code*. IPADE has clout in Mexico, said by those who go there to be "the Harvard Business School of Mexico."

Armando gained further height from his love of men's suits, which he wore even when he was not at weddings or work. They distinguished him, identified him with his kind. And they disguised him as they connected him to an office somewhere off the street, one that, at this moment, he didn't have. But he didn't want people to know that.

AT SOME POINT during Armando's rekindling of what he thought were life-sustaining relationships, the five-inch-thick, fifteen-foot-tall, hand-carved church doors, darkened with age to the color of dark roasted coffee, opened on their arm-sized, wrought iron hinges. There were hundreds of us now being shepherded through them and into the church's entranceway. From there and in couples we were ushered down the sixteenth-century, cathedral-ceiling nave and into the pews where we sat, now quiet, like little human specks overshadowed by the grandeur. We were surrounded on our sides and to our back by the cold interior walls of Aztec-quarried stone, dismantled from one kind of pyramid and repositioned into another by indigenous laborers under Spanish rule. The larger-than-life iconography was bathed in the music coming from the choir, which the Classical Orchestra of Mexico City, hired for the occasion, had begun to play. The choir floated above the last few pews in the back, making it difficult to see the players from where we sat. That was on purpose because the music that came from it was sung by angels, who joined in a remarkable way with the clerestory light that filtered through the stained glass above it. Over it all, the church's arched and enclosed heavens floated.

I thought then about the word *cielo*, which means ceiling (*cielo raso*), sky, and heaven all wrapped up in one, expanding on the Latin neuter *caelum*,[2] heaven and sky, from which it came. Sometimes cielo is used affectionately to refer to someone meaningful in one's life, "mi cielo" or "cielo mío," translating into my sky, my heaven, my angel, my love, my glory that arches over me or arches over someone else, a blessed child, a sweetheart, a sweetie pie, *un cielo lindo*. I thought of the evolution of the Spanish language from Latin, and how it came into its own and matured simultaneously with the building of great, stone cathedrals in Spain.

The interior walls of the outside-in pyramid of Churubusco were adorned with replicas and reliquaries, suspended above eye level, of the Virgin of Guadalupe, Saint Francis of Assisi, Saint Mary of the Angels, the Purist of Conceptions, and the relics of one or two saints. In front were clusters of votive candles, the lit ones still beating the heartwarming prayers composed and whispered that morning by loved ones. A Mexican flag stood over to the side to remind parishioners that the State owned and curated all churches in Mexico, as established by the 1917 Constitution. Although after so many decades of State ownership, the flag's presence in them seemed like a symbol of partnership rather than proprietorship, which is why, perhaps, Salinas left that relationship alone. In the back were murals of the Stations of the Cross, and at the two ends of the transept that traversed before the pulpit were secondary altars in gold with a small collection of pews facing them.

Over the next two hours the wedding ceremony that Armando wanted me to witness unfolded along a tightly scripted narrative with well-rehearsed staging. It was a Mexican, upper-class, Catholic variation on an ancient and worldwide tradition, where the exchange of wealth and the alliance of families are often central to the wedding story. In this case, very central. As were the expected maternity of the virgin bride and paternity of the groom, united for no higher purpose, in the paraphrased words of the priest.

MANY YEARS LATER looking back on the event, I wrote to Armando to ask him what he remembered of that day. He remembered every one of the who's who. He could recount their names, their relationships to one another, and their positions in the business world, a vast kinship chart made of discretions and indiscretions and reinforced with balloons of mortared gossip. He also remembered the famous singer at the reception.

I, on the other hand, was able to recount everything else, probably because unfamiliarity is alerting, as is self-consciousness. Along with the setting I remembered each of the ten-course dishes served, the champagne that flowed, the wines that were poured, the baked Alaska that arrived flaming for all five hundred dinner guests. How could I forget that? And during our reminiscing, I began to feel the shoes, the wrong shoes, I had worn. Not that I have ever been well-heeled, but one or two pairs for all occasions was not going to work well in my line of research back then among wealthy politicians and art gallery goers. However, I couldn't bring myself to carry to Mexico more than one small suitcase. Finally, I remembered being the only one out of five hundred guests to have never learned the tango.

I had kept a vivid picture in my mind for all these years of the bride, in her creamy white, nineteenth-century dress of French Georgette silk and Brussels lace that she had bought in Paris and had had embroidered with hundreds of rose pearls from the sea. Also in the archives of my mind sat motionless and in basic black the congregation, a shadowy, evening backdrop to the bride's rising, crescent moon. In my mind I could still see the ecclesiastical vestments of the priest, the chalice used for the Holy Communion and the handkerchief the priest used to wipe it clean, because to me it didn't seem germ-swiping enough, and I had a vivid memory of the moment the choir sang Handel's Hallelujah chorus. That's when the bride and groom turned around, and with a final blessing from the priest and surrounded by the choir's angelic praises of Christ's resurrection and God's triumph, they walked down the aisle, out the church, and into the night.

I saved the newspaper articles as well as the notes I had written about it. These helped where my memory failed. At the time I did not think the wedding was more than an entertaining diversion from my proposed focus on art and politics. I had taken notes because, as a student of anthropology, I had been trained to do so. You never know when you might need some information that at the time of noting may seem miles from your current mission, anthropologists Louise Lamphere and Dwight Heath had counseled me.

That turned out to be good guidance not only for the more immediate task of my dissertation way back when, but for my growing obsession over the years to understand madre. With the help of good hardy notes and some calls to Armando, I began to connect the dots.

I first drew a line from the virgin bride to the Virgin Mother. It was easy and direct. They had faced each other for almost two hours during the ceremony, the Virgin at the altar, the bride and groom in front of her. From there, I drew another line to *ambivalent*, the adjective I decided best described the list of madres I had accrued, an adjective my list continued to exhibit as it lengthened.

Then I drew a line to *irreconcilable*, because it's practically impossible for any bride to live up to the Virgin's grace. For as miraculous as it was for the Virgin Mother to have earned her title, it is equally oxymoronic for any bride to reconcile that title with her own married-with-children life that will inevitably follow her wedding day. If mortal mothers cannot be virgins *and* biological mothers simultaneously, a basic fact of human reproduction, how can they emulate the Virgin Mother, which contemporary Church teachings encourage them to do? It may not have been this bride's goal at all to reconcile this dilemma, or any Mexican bride's. Not one of my Mexican friends or acquaintances who is a mother ever thinks of herself in terms of the Virgin, although she sometimes points to others who she *knows* do. But the iconography of the Church is hard to escape while you are within its range, and its range, as I had seen all over town in statues and statuettes, extends way beyond the church and into taxis and buses and newspapers and private altars inside homes and gardens—and even into the secular iconography of the State.

From *ambivalent* and the *Virgin* I drew a line to *Eve*, the first mother of the human race, according to the Bible. This connected the two most well-known madres in the Catholic pantheon of mothers. Eve, however, is the bad mother. She is so bad that Catholic children all over the world are baptized to rid themselves of the original sin that she and Adam committed. Eve gave into temptation, and Adam followed her lead. The Virgin would never have done that. She would never have gone against God's will. Nor would she have tempted others to do so.

And by drawing a line from the *Virgin* to *Eve*, I also connected the eye of the storm with the storm itself, so that the serene, indoor opulence of the church, connected to the outdoors, where the impatience of everyday urban commotion and the agitation of its sinners carried out the rituals of everyday life. It was out there where I collected those madres and made my lists at night.

From these two mothers and their environments, I swung back and forth for a while, immortal to mortal, pure to dangerous, virtuous to easily tempted, good to bad. What kept the two mothers apart, and the dualities that they symbolized meaningful, were the moral teachings that they characterized: a narrative means for children, both boys and girls, to carry in their minds two categories of mothers; moral lessons for staying on the straight and narrow; but, also, a sensibility for using madre expressions later in life and having them mean something—having them work, both effectively and affectively, on oneself and others.

The sensibility was complicated, of course. One complication that came to mind immediately was found in the creation narratives that accompanied the Virgin and Eve. These are narratives that are placed outside the normal experience of maternity. In Eve's case it is her own birth from Adam, and in the Virgin's case it is the virgin conception of her son. In both stories the normal course of events, which would have occurred had these been stories of ordinary people, would have had Eve give birth to Adam and the Mother of Jesus to have conceived and given birth without remaining a virgin.

Another complication arose from the church narratives of fathers, both the pure and celibate church fathers and all other fathers, the latter who were no more chaste than the mother of their children were virgins. And there was the Mexican flag, the symbol of the paternalistic State, that draped over Virgins and flew atop church buildings all over Mexico. There were dots in these padre narratives that in my mind were looking around for a connection to madre. After all, boys and men are the largest users of the madre expressions. Might there be several reasons for this? But I couldn't connect them just then.

"Armando?"

"Yes."

I was thinking that all over the world groups of people have their ways to insult mothers or use mothers to insult others. With beer-drinking buddies there are the *motherfuckers*, among African Americans there are the *yo mamas*, and with children, *Your mother is ugly*, to give three examples from the United States. But Mexico, I learned soon enough, has had a corner on the North and South American markets of mother insults for a long time, going way beyond simple noun phrases.

"What's here in Mexican Spanish that is not there in English or in the rest of the Spanish-speaking world, for that matter?" I asked, after summarizing the dots I had connected so far.

He agreed I had a good point.

"You agree?"

Maybe it was his long-distance view of things, sitting in the living room of his London flat with his laptop on the dining room table. Maybe it was his arrival at middle age or the English we sometimes used or the *tamal* I held up to my computer's camera to show him what I was having for lunch, as I sat in the kitchen of my current rental in Mexico. For whatever reason, Armando was starting to have opinions about madre. They weren't flooding our conversations, but they were beginning to trickle in.

LOOKING BACK ON the wedding again, not to mention the numerous other tours and detours all around town that I took with Armando when we were young, it was clear to me now. Had it not been for the haywire circuitry of his tireless avoidance of the madre topic, where the shortest distance between two points was never going to be the route we traveled, I might not have ventured to notice the extent to which madre was having affairs with referents other than her own. And not only religious ones, but plenty of secular ones, too.

Also, reminiscing about my adventures with Armando made me recall the three essential translation questions that the Chinese scholar Achilles Fang once raised. The first and second were standard, with regard to how well the translator understands the original text and how well she or he converts it into another. However the third was concerned with the in between.

"But what happens in between?" the writer Forrest Gander asked, when contemplating Fang's essential questions in a meditation of his, concerning the translation of Spanish poetry into English.[3]

"Well, for one," I thought to myself while reading his essay, "car rides with Armando."

LOVE

PABLO whispered in my ear, "A *mamacita* or a fuckup." And then, doubling over in his laughter, added directly what the others hadn't, "An educated woman like you should not be talking about such things!"

I first met Pablo in Providence, Rhode Island, where I was teaching linguistic anthropology at Brown University in the first half of the 1990s. We were at a reunion of Mexican writers who had gathered in the lobby of the Hispanic Studies Department. He was an investigative reporter, rather than a politician like Armando. That's not to say he's indiscreet. It's just that he likes to uncover more than cover up, in his case, inconsistencies, scandals, government lies, and the like. Yet in our friendship, it is I who have relentlessly pursued him to fill me in on this madre matter.

"Could you explain that more?" I asked him, time and again, mentioning, on occasion, what I had learned in between about madre. "For example, *A toda madre* or *un desmadre* is like everything is perfect, paradise, like all of your mother's love. Or it's hell," I told him, paraphrasing some lines from the 1993 movie *Blood In, Blood Out*. I mentioned the time that I, along with ten others, had tea and tacos with Mexican writer Carlos Fuentes, who, when hearing about my interests in the matter, added a few more madres, such as *esas madres* and *poca madre*, to my list, intoning them various ways and laughing all the while, yet leaving them undefined.

"I don't know how I can put this in plain words for you, but expressions with *madre* in them are *fuertes*, powerful," he would deliberate, his repeated warning laced with laughter.

"But Pablo, I'm an anthropologist," I would push on.

And so it's been, these interchanges having taken place in person, by phone, and by email, in the same or in different countries. Ever since.

Sometimes he wrote from his home in Guadalajara, his left fist wrapped around a shot of whiskey while he typed with his free index finger. "It can be dangerous to say *madre* in Mexico." Underscored and italicized. His words would blow fire across the screen. A kind of watch-out *fuerte*, not only powerful, but really powerful. Like a match to gasoline, or a blow to the face.

I pictured him seated on the wooden chair at his desk, where I had seen him before, his back to the room, his ruggedly handsome face like that of a professorial Dennis Quaid. The air still in his walk-up apartment, which was sparse compared to the house he left behind with his wife and son: a couch, a chair, a desk, a lamp. Windows opened. A coolness outside, cooler than the dry, hot days, when the dust whirls through the streets. A stack of newspapers and journals on the far corner of the desk, cascading onto the floor.

I knew what he was wearing. For as long as I have known him he has worn the same wrinkle-free uniform: a pair of well-ironed blue jeans, a starched white cotton shirt opened at the neck, sleeves buttoned at the wrist. He never rolled his sleeves up like U.S. male journalists do around the world. On his feet he wore his favorite cowboy boots, recently polished, which were his Guadalajara and masculine trademark, even though the city's cowboy days had long ago passed. While he wrote he was no doubt well shaven, without glasses or contacts.

"Madre?" I wrote back, from my computer in Mexico City,

"the noun, mother? How can mother, the very source of safety, be considered dangerous?" I challenged in response.

"Esas madres. *Those* mothers," Pablo responded, trying to explain to me *these* from *those* in journalistic prose.

I began to learn Spanish in my early twenties. I have never had an ear for music or any sense of rhythm. Had I learned the language as a child, I might have circumvented these obstacles, but by adulthood, and with a well-formed larynx descended into place, I was operating against the odds. Also, I interpret novelty literally, or I did until Spanish—or Mexicans—eventually changed me. But before that, my literalness was another hurdle.

When Pablo issued his warning, I was reminded of a handbook I had sought out at one point on Mexican Spanish. It suggested that in Mexico it was better to avoid saying the word *madre* altogether. Make inquiries instead about a person's *mamá* rather than his or her *madre*.[1] It was safer, it warned. Elsewhere in Latin America, it wasn't so. How's your madre? Chileans and Colombians, Argentines and Costa Ricans ask. But in Mexico? Shhhh. Invisible index fingers are raised to silent hissing lips. "Don't say that word."

"Esas madres, *those* mothers," Pablo repeated.

Pablo had been invited to Brown, to a conference on Mexican writers, that included Carlos Fuentes, Elena Poniatowska, and Carmen Boullosa among others. Something about the way he smiled at the gathering in the lobby and his being out of context inspired me to drive him around the city with his shopping list, a ritual I had performed many times with visitors to the university. Shopping lists can tell you a lot about a visitor and his or her country of origin. With other Mexicans before him, it was usually the latest variation of Barbie—the white one, not the Latina one—blue jeans made in the U.S., anything from GAP, and other items of fashion, pleasure, or leisure unavailable in Mexico at the time. This was before the North American Free Trade Agreement, and, also, before China. With Pablo, it was mostly computer paraphernalia and office supplies.

We had not gone a block when Pablo asked me my age and my income. I was used to Mexicans asking me these questions in Mexico. My "outsider" status caused all sorts of otherwise taboo questions to be raised. But we weren't in Mexico. He said he'd never met a university professor who looked like me—a makeup-less woman in her thirties sporting a baseball cap worn backward, hair fashioned into a ponytail, which disappeared under the sloping visor. By his standards, I hardly resembled a student, let alone a professor.

I told Pablo, pointing to myself, not to judge *this* book by its cover, that, while I kept it a secret most of the time, I knew about elegance. "I'll have you know," I proudly asserted, "that, while I may not look the part currently, I have been elegant. On occasion."

He gave me that look—Oh, really?—as though he didn't believe a word I said.

To set him straight I explained that I had spent time in the company of the most elegant women I could think of in matters of poise and style—the women of Mexico City, who were professors, lawyers, politicians, gallery dealers, the wives and daughters of wealthy families. I mentioned Armando's Hispanophile mother, who called me Linda Preciosa, by the way. But, it's true. Not long after my initial arrival in Mexico City I had come to accept the fact that, at least in this life, I would never have the look, gait, gesture, hair, or fingernails to be a member of that particular elegance-elite club, those who always appeared effortlessly impeccable, no matter what time of day or context, those who spoke French when in Paris, English when in Dallas. But I had achieved some success at assimilation among my failures, thank you very much.

I had, for instance, learned to drop my voice half an octave, as Mexico's elegant women do when they speak. Their maids speak at a higher register, one or two octaves up. I had learned to raise my voice on the first syllable of *villa*, pronounced beé·ya, when moved to exclaim, "Qué maravilla" as I stood with these women in front of paintings by well-known local artists. Something equivalent to a lockjawed, "Simply marvelous." And when I did this for Pablo, he howled. I'm not sure if he was laughing at me or with me. I forgot to ask.

I told him that in the two years I had lived there and during the two that followed, when I commuted back and forth from Providence, I took to imitating not only the cadence and tone, but also the grammar of the elegant Mexican women's Spanish. I adopted the subjunctive with abandon and "¿No, sí? and ¿Sí, no?" setting aside any personal or cultural need to pin things down. Is it yes or is it no? I didn't know, although I began to develop a sense for one or the other. And I was pretty sure they knew. But it did not seem to matter either way.

Emboldened by my lingual success, I attempted to conquer the visual. I grew, and even painted, my fingernails, and I put on the classiest graduate-student dress I owned. I straightened my posture and let my blonde hair down. When Armando was unavailable, I hired a driver to wait for me. This helped my status. But I come from a family of short people, and elegant Mexicans are tall. So on occasion I slipped into what, for me, were high heels. Of course they were low compared to the three-inch standards of Mexico, worn everywhere, even up and down the narrow and numerous precipitous steps of the pyramids of Teotihuacan, an archaeological site an hour north of the city. One woman, I'll never forget, with a baby in her arms. I'm not kidding.

It is true, however, that elegance did not come easily. Once, prior to a gallery opening, when Armando's sister and niece arrived to collect me and had decided in unison to do something about my colorless face, they pulled from their handbags large makeup bags, out of which they produced the necessary tools for my transformation. They applied dark mascara to my pale eyelashes and eyebrows, a wide swath of black eyeliner around my slate blue eyes, and a ruby red gloss to my no-lips in an effort to have me pass for a native at the party that followed. Had I been a dark-eyed, tall brunette with a different outfit, I might have. But I looked instead like a transvestite. Only not even that good because I had never quite mastered the art of walking on stilettos.

Also, while we're on the topic of elegance, these elegant women were all mothers and I wasn't, not back then. Motherhood in Mexico really ups your status, if you are among the elegant women, anyway. Not looking maternal or announcing it physically, but referring to your children on occasion, the way married women, when among women, refer to having a husband when they feel they need some elevation. Of course, children can lower your status elsewhere in the mother hierarchy. Too many, too poor, for example. No husband to name drop.

It was Pablo, not I, who was out of his element his first visit to Providence. So I reminded him when asked my age that he was in Rome, and in New England the Romans don't ask that question of women. Then I attempted an explanation of why New Englanders also avoided talking about money. But when we spoke in Spanish, I bargained with him. "I'll tell you my age and my salary if you come clean with me on esas madres" and a few other speech utterances about men and women's body parts that, I had been told by a fellow anthropologist, had gurgled up the class ladder from the bars and street corners of the barrio and from one group of men to another group of men, although I never found evidence for that assertion, which I now believe to be stigma rather than historical fact.[2] I knew they were going over my head when I had the opportunity to hear them. I also knew it wasn't proper for me to be discussing them, Armando had been clear with me on that.

And sure enough, that's when Pablo issued his warning.

"You must watch what you say, where, how, and to whom you say it."

Madre was not to be taken literally, according to Pablo. "In Mexico it doesn't mean 'mother' most of the time. And by the way, *No es propio de una mujer educada como tu . . .* It isn't appropriate for an educated woman such as yourself to talk of those things."

His hesitation with my questions, not the impropriety of my

questions but the discomfort of his having to discuss such a culturally improper subject matter with a "lady," made me relentless. I
egged him on.

"I'm an anthropologist, for heaven's sake . . ."

"¡Okey, okey!" He once wrote in an email to me. It was the
summer of 1994, less than six months before the end of Carlos
Salinas's sexenio, the one-time-only, six-year term allowed him.
Pablo was enraged at the situation his country was in. Instead
of groping for examples of how people might use *madre*, he just
released his anger out loud, unfiltered, as if he were talking to a
male buddy.

Salinas's presidency had been tumultuous, and it included lots of
high-profile murders, voter fraud, random violence, and suspect,
economic packages that involved family and friends. As violence
was going up, prices were going up, interest rates were going
up, rents were going up, and drug dealing was going up, but the
standard of living was going down. Except for the drug dealers'
standard of living, and that of some politicians.

So instead of helping me out with the meaning of *those* madres,
all Pablo could do, during our car rides about the city of Providence
and later via many email interchanges, was use them. He neither
explained them, nor dissected them, because he really needed to
use them right then.

"Sorry for not writing earlier. I've been distracted trying to
understand why what has happened in this country, in such a short
time, has happened." He apologized in an email to me. "Nos carga
la chingada." (We are being carried by the fucked one, that is, the
government is fucking us over, treating us like a whore.)

I imagined an arabesque of smoke abandoning the cigarette that
most definitely hung from his mouth. It rose slowly, caught a twirl
of air, then looped around once, twice, before rolling into the rays
of light falling from a bulb that dangled at the end of a black wire
in the center of the room. There was the sound of a keyboard. A
shot or two of whiskey to take off the edge.

Chingar was a big word in twentieth century Mexico and is still a big word in twenty-first-century Mexico, I learned after talking to Pablo. It is tied directly to madre, he explained. It means to fuck or rape, and goes like this: *chingada*, past participle with the feminine ending *-a*, a woman who is fucked or raped, a whore. Expressions that go from there are *Chinga tu madre* (fuck your mother, meaning fuck you), *hijo de tu puta madre* (son of a bitch, son of your whore bitch mother), *tu chingada madre* (your fucked mother), *tu madre* (your mother). Sometimes there's no need for *chingada*, people will know on most occasions. Or keep *chingada*, leave out *madre*. Each is powerful enough on its own.[3]

He clarified: "A Catholic cardinal and presidential candidate murdered, burned ballots, a contested election, a swift rise to power, more peso devaluations, soaring interest rates, more capital flight, corporate scandals, more murders, a rise in drug trafficking."

After twenty years as a journalist covering Mexican politics in Mexico City from his office in Guadalajara, Pablo ventured into being the director of a new magazine that mixed culture with politics and maintained an outsider perspective, outside Mexico City, the capital of presidential power and, in the minds of most of the city's intelligentsia, the center for everything in Mexico.

Guadalajara, Mexico's second largest city, located in the state of Jalisco, is a six-hour drive northwest of *El D.F.*, the Federal District, as Mexico City is known. Its name derives from the Arabic, *wadii al-Hajara*, which translates into the "Valley of Stones," a name the Spaniards gave to the area. A certain spiky blue agave cactus loves to grow in these stones, so not far outside Guadalajara in the town of Tequila, one of the world's best drinks is produced. And because over 6 million people reside in Guadalajara's greater metropolitan area, Pablo felt compelled to ask publicly: Why does Mexico City dominate everything in Mexico? What happened to Mexico's "periphery"? What of the arts in Guadalajara and in other Mexican cities? What of Guadalajara's perspective on the relationship of Mexico to the U.S., free trade, border politics, and Mexican emigration? What can be said of Chicano film, art, and literature? And, most important, why wasn't a multicentered political system possible in Mexico? These were all topics ignored by Mexico City intellectual elite back then. He didn't like Mexico City's dominance one bit.

"Not everything is covered by the federal politicians' rhetoric or the Mexico City newspapers that serve them. Or critique them. Not everything is in Mexico City. There *are* other points of view in Mexico," he wrote. "The general feeling around here in Guadalajara is of having been profoundly deceived and mocked by the President and his team of technocrats. *El país les vale madre,* the country is worth a mother. That is, *to them*, the country is worthless and they don't give a damn about it."

"Worthless?" I reacted as though I had not heard the *me vale madre* expression before.

"No, the country," he returned, "and because of this, they have caused a *desmadre*, a fuckup, a disaster, a catastrophe."

"A disaster, *des-madre*?" I asked. And on hearing the word, rather than seeing and picturing it, I thought that if *vale madre*, to be worth a mother, is to be worthless, then *des-madre* should mean the opposite of that. "Because *des-madre* translates into 'not having' [*des*] a 'mother' [*madre*], right?" I asked again. "And that can be catastrophic because, as I see it, mothers are worth something here."

And then I explained to Pablo how I was thinking what I was thinking, which went like this. "For example, is it that the *des* of *desmadre* is a prefix like *de, dis, des* in English that *reverses* the meaning of the root it precedes, like decriminalize? Or *removes* the root as in deoxygenate, meaning to take the oxygen out? Or *reduces* its importance as in declassify? In other words, is *des-madre*, *madre*-deoxygenated, *madre* with the wind taken out of her? Does *des* take out the *madre*, remove the order, the oxygen, the goodness and leave a disorderly life, the life one has without a mother?

The way children's bedrooms or the daily menu or daily routines become after she's left? Like a government without a mother?"

He wasn't sure.

"Or, wait a minute. Was it the other way around?"

So I wrote back with a complete opposite idea from my earlier one. Then explained my reversed direction. "Did the *des* of *desmadre* intensify the root, instead of cancel the root out? For example, take disannul, which simply means to annul, but really, really. Or, along the same line, indicate the malevolence of a root, as in disaster, which literally means the malevolence of an aster, an aster being a kind of star found inside a cell."

It must be the former, I thought to myself, as I waited for his response.

"A fuckup," Pablo wrote back.

"And what's a fuckup," I asked him, "if not an accidental child?" But I kept thinking, More of a mother or less of one? Too much and so a dis-aster? Or not enough, and, so dis-order, dis-ease?

"A fuckup." Pablo repeated.

I WENT BACK to Mexico City for most summers in the 1990s. The July air was always heavy in the mornings with a haze that the dry earth, the seasonal winds, and the factories to the north in combination with millions of old vehicles created. But after the rains washed through it for an hour or two each day in the early afternoon, it cleared and became transparent again. Crossing the streets at this time was awful because it was hard to escape the current of water that formed after so much rain in such a short time. Whenever I stepped into the thick, slurpy stream, filled with the dust and grime laundered from the sullied air, my leather shoes became drenched, along with those of all the other pedestrians anxious to get to where we had planned to go that day. I remember wishing I'd had my rubber boots that people in Maine, where I now live, wear, and not the elegant shoes Mexican society required women to wear. Instead, wet feet formed part of my life and memories during the rainy season in Mexico City.

In the evenings, when the streets were quiet, I would usually correspond with Pablo. As I waited for his response to my latest inquiry—these were the slow days of dial up—I whiled away the time clipping the newspaper articles that remained unread from the morning papers. I saved articles I thought useful to my interest in art and politics. I also saved articles for no particular reason, other than that I found them curiously strange, worth remembering for storytelling later. I filed them in individual folders, each containing the various newspapers' take on a particular event.

One such file was labeled "padre," father. I took the articles out to browse, perhaps for the distraction but also to jog my memory. Inside the file there were clippings titled, "Penetración Cultural." Another "Garbage King Murdered." They were dated 1987. I remembered the events. The first belonged to a collection of clippings I had made with that title. The use of "penetration" to describe unwanted foreign influence in Mexico was so prevalent that I stopped saving examples. But when I first saw them, they struck me. There was no escaping the sexualized nature of the term, not only because *pene*, the word for penis, began it, but, when illustrated, *La Nación*, the Nation, was drawn as a violated woman.

Then I picked up the second article, on the murder. At the time my friends and I speculated whether it was a political murder. Or was it a love affair gone wrong? The evidence was inside a biography of intrigue, of marriages, divorces, lovers, and children galore, and in the photographs that hung on the Garbage King's office wall of political handshakes and airborne kisses.

When the story broke, I had gone to the dump with the journalist Jane Bussey a few days after the murder. She loved, and still loves, investigative reporting. It led her to uncover juicy facts that often made her unpopular. Also, it made her phone not work a lot. When it worked it was tapped. And mine, too, because of our friendship, I presumed. Whenever she invited me to join her, I did. And then my phone had issues. Along the mile-long, winding road leading up the dump, guards armed with machine guns patrolled the way.

As the story unfolded, we learned that at stake were the following: a fiefdom; a rigid hierarchy of relationships; a lot of tribute, kickbacks, and paybacks. At the bottom were thirty thousand *pepenadores*, garbage pickers, who separated the bones from the glass, the cans from the food, the aluminum from the cardboard, and after eating what was left on the bones, they sold the piles of recyclables to the King. They were beholden to him. The King, in turn, was beholden to the city's mayor, who was beholden to the ruling Party or some political bosses somewhere, who were beholden to a complex of quid pro quos that circled back to the King who provided the instant crowds needed by the then-ruling Institutional Revolutionary Party for political rallies. And now in his absence, who was beholden to whom? And which wife, lover, child was now going to start shaking hands and with whom?

I had filed these articles under "padre" because what had astounded me about the story at one point was not so much the machine guns or the indentured labor, the money that exchanged hands, the fact that there was a king of garbage, but that this man had proudly claimed to have sired one hundred children.[4] Now in retrospect and with a rereading, I thought of him as a metonym, a limb, a hand, a foot, some appendage of the paternalistic patriarchy of the Mexican state. So I put the articles back under "padre," and returned to thinking about madre and whether Pablo had responded, which he had.

"*Ahora que nos dieron en la madre*, we are telling the government and the ruling party, *que se vayan chingar a su madre*. Am I making myself clear?"

"No," I wrote, as I struggled with a translation. Now that the government gave it to us in the mother, gave it to us in our weak spot or our strong spot, kicked us in our privates or all over our bodies, now that the politicos have fucked us over, we the Mexican people are telling the government and the ruling party, to go fuck their mothers.

"Are privates madres?" At this point I was really getting lost.

"No."

He continued: "The history of Mexico will someday note that the politicians of the 20th century, *que no tuvieron madre*" (who had no mother, meaning no manners, no culture), "left the country in the worst bankruptcy ever. Of course, that is no more than a small consolation for future generations. For all of us right now, however, we'll just have to put up with the *desmadre*, the fuckup, and work super hard. Is it possible for us to work even harder than we do now? So that *no nos carge la chingada*" (So that they don't stick us with the fucking mother). "I mean, so they don't *kill* us. Our unscrupulous leaders *se están llevando el país a la chingada*" (are taking the country to the fucking mother, are putting us in real trouble right now). "And they are fucking up Mexico."

"Dear Pablo," I wrote back immediately. "It can't be this simple can it, that *those madres* are fucked, and *these madres* are not?" I meant it literally. I didn't want to get into the worn-out, virgin-whore flip-flop, explaining women's problems in Mexico with that model. But in situ, impromptu ire is not known for being complex and nuanced. It's generally pretty basic. Raw, rather than cooked. So I asked, "Are *these* mothers different from *those* because of you-know-what?" He knew I was thinking about sex. Although I'm not sure he knew that I was also thinking of rape.

WHEN I WROTE again to Pablo he was still in shock over the politics of his countrymen, and, also, toiling to keep his magazine alive. In those days he worked into the early hours of the morning, every morning. Each issue was imaginative and gorgeous. The articles were not by or about the usual suspects.

"I don't know what's going to happen to this country," he continued with his earlier thoughts.

Looking back on it now I can see that he felt helpless. The government had insulted his mother, his origins, his very being. How was he to respond appropriately and legally? Well, with language. He had no choice.

"Or you respond physically, with a *madrazo*, a big jolt, a mother of a blow," Pablo added once.

"Madrazo, huh? Anyway, how do you do that if it's the government hurling the daggers?" I asked him.

"You can't. So you're fucked," he said, and meant his mother's fucked. Or your mother. Then went for a walk.

He stepped into a liquor store, bought a bottle of tequila *reposado*, but not without eyeing the *añejo*, his favorite kind with its golden glow after aging a full year. It was worth the price, but he didn't have it. He went home and poured the long tradition of distilled blue *agave* into his glass, securing his roots in the stony valley of his birth. Music shuddered through the open window, an all-night party in the neighborhood. A rooster on someone's rooftop crowed before daybreak, he had some *madres* to say about that, under the laundry, washed and hung, blowing in the early morning breeze.

He sat down again to write, his fingers on the keyboard, tongue back in his cheek. Between the lines I saw him smiling, almost laughing as if he were with his buddies in the bar singing *rancheras* about lost loves. Sadness drowned by the joy of being sad together and by the brass instruments that always blast out these songs. Not like men who listened to tangos in the early morning bars of Buenos Aires, contemplative and solitary, while the *bandoneón* inhaled and exhaled the heavy air back into the room.

No, not like Argentines.

Like Mexicans.

With a pathos that *pica* like a jalapeño. Only not just any bite, a loud and mockingly joyful one—with trumpets.

That evening I turned on my computer and there was a message from Pablo.

"Unfortunately, no one can imagine that everything in Mexico will ever return to being a *padre*, a father, to being magnificent. Will Mexico ever be a magnificent father again? Ordered, the politicians honest, income steady, interest rates down, inflation down, peso up, movies thought provoking, the press free, journalists safe, streets secure. If, in fact, it was even ever that way in the first place."

"Magnificent?" I asked when I read his mail. "Father?"

"Yes. Why?"

"Well," and I explained it to him with a question. "*Esas madres* are worthless because they are fucked, and fathers are magnificent because they you-know-what in the active voice?" I thought of the Garbage King.

"You're still too literal."

Pablo drank the tequila. It probably burned as he used to say it did, but in a good way. The way hot peppers unhinge the eyes, set the tongue on fire, drive heat down the spine. A burn that warms as it warns. He checked the midnight oil and returned to work on the magazine, still believing that it would succeed.

THE NEXT SUMMER Pablo came to visit me in Maine. I was renting a small cabin on the shores of the New Meadows River, a tidal, saltwater river that feeds into the rocky coast. He fell in love with the poetry of its description and, with absolutely no thought, hopped on a plane to Boston where I picked him up. With so little expendable income and with the declining economic situation in Mexico, he told me that he thought he must be crazy.

I had mentioned to him, months earlier, something about the sun shower at high noon and the rainbows inside each drop of water that cascaded from the opened spout; the freshwater eel from the Sargasso Sea lurking behind a fallen stone at the bottom of the covered spring where I fetched the day's water; the fireflies in the field at night, each with its unique luminescent Morse-code signal, yet all translating into a single message: Hey, over here, I'm the one. I mentioned the ruby-throated hummingbirds and

Monarch butterflies, how they may winter in Mexico, but they summer in Maine.

We sang *ranchera* music with the sunroof opened, Lola Beltrán in the CD player with a full mariachi band to help me stay on key, and the moon above us as we made our way up the coast with the downeast summer winds behind us that August evening.

He's right, I thought. He is crazy.

The next morning, I showed him how to hoist the bag of hot water warmed by the heat of the morning sun up the south side of the cabin and above his head with the pulley system devised by the last tenant, and then to bathe between lobster boats which came by twice a day with bearded men and strong women in big, yellow rubber pants held up by wide, black suspenders, to check the traps. His modesty was challenged. He had thought my earlier reference describing the sun shower was poetry, not prose. He wasn't in the least bit countercultural, he told me, nor had he ever been—or would he ever be—a hippie. But he adapted quickly when I served him lobster for breakfast, lunch, and dinner.

I fell in love with Pablo. It was his sense of humor. His smile. His passion in challenging Mexico City's hegemony. And, if truth be told, his cowboy boots. Maybe even the fact he ironed his jeans, which was the piece I found most foreign about him. But he had a wife back home, and also a girlfriend. And, he said, we could never be lovers anyway because he respected me too much. I thought maybe we couldn't because he was busy. Not at all. He was protecting me from becoming one of *those madres* because he really liked me. He was even in love with me.

Two years later, somewhat recovered from his trip to Maine and the literal sun showers he endured there, Pablo headed south from Guadalajara to see me in Mexico City. Salinas was out of office and Zedillo, his successor, was trying to stabilize the malaise and chaos his predecessor and *cuates* (buddies) had caused. He wasn't successful. I was in Mexico to give a lecture to Brown alumni in Citibank's conference room located on the top floor of a tall building on the business end of Reforma, not far from the Zona Rosa, a center of fancy shops and nightclubs. It was luxurious.

When I came to live in Mexico City two years after the devastating earthquake of 1985, the tall buildings that lined this part of Reforma formed a double row of tree-lined gravestones. It was a haunting sight: twelve-story buildings, cracked up their sides and down their middles, some leaning against others; windows shattered and gone. Elsewhere in the city underground and unknown prisons were revealed by the toppled edifices, as were building contracts given to brothers and uncles with little regard for the engineering required of Mexico's plate-shifting geography and soft lakebed above it. But in the nineties, it was all cleaned up. Little evidence of the horror that struck remained on this central boulevard.

We made plans to meet the next day. But when he left the building he was mugged after getting in a cab, robbed, and left for dead on a sidewalk elsewhere in the city. I did not know what had happened until I returned to Providence. I received an email from him, filled with a lot of esas madres, a lot of motherfuckers. Because some thugs had been fucking with him by way of his mother.

TWELVE YEARS HAVE passed since the last time I saw Pablo. Two presidents have come into office with promises of change and two have left, their promises unfulfilled. The jury's out with the current one. During these changing administrations Pablo, whom I first met when he was in his late thirties, has turned forty, forty-five, and now fifty-something. He became a grandfather shortly after the twenty-first century commenced. And I fell in love with another man, then out of love, then back in love with another, became a mother of twins and then a single mother of twins. During all that, I carried a torch for Pablo. He has sent me photographs of the little guy. I have responded with pictures of my midlife crises. I avoid pictures of myself, although when I'm feeling like Julius Caesar, who, as he aged, sent younger images of himself to mint into commemorative coins, I send early photographs of me from back in the days when I used to sleep. Now that I'm trying to write this book, I started up again with my *"madre* questions," and "What's your take on the political situation now?" which provoke him to this day.

And I love that.

I guess he doesn't mind it. He hasn't stopped responding, and with his tongue in his cheek just as before. But he's now older and wiser and jaded. And, I sense, heartbroken.

After eight years fighting to make a different voice for Mexico, Pablo's magazine failed. He became a teacher at the university in Guadalajara to make ends meet and continued to write for newspapers in the area. Mexico's economic situation became worse. While there were fewer political assassinations, there were more random murders by police, taxi drivers, and street thugs. A surge of kidnappings, disappearances, continue to this day, escalating in most areas. Some places are entirely under siege.

While reading two autumns ago that 46 percent of all Mexicans wanted to leave the country and move to the United States, up from 41 percent the previous February, the statistics did not surprise him. Promises from the federal government that the situation will improve are hollow and, for the hardworking, opportunities at home are even fewer than before. The poor and the not-so-poor want to improve their lot in life. Not all of them want to become drug dealers and kidnappers. Who can blame them? So hoping for something better, they leave. Those who stay behind wait for those who left to send money, return in December for the Virgin's birthday, come see their children and their *abuelitas*, their grandmothers, who care for the left-behind children as they would all other gifts from heaven.

But Pablo?

He's staying put. Some day Mexico might, indeed, be padre again, and he's hoping to witness it.

"I'm focused on an unlikely miracle, aren't I?" He asked in one of his meditations to me.

It was a rhetorical question I assumed, but found myself nodding because along with youth, optimism slips away, too, after a while.

Meanwhile he has knowledge and thoughts about the government's shenanigans, which he will continue to publish. He's a journalist. It's his calling. He's not backing down. And, anyway, you've probably figured it out by now that his printed stories are his madrazos. They are the mothers-of-a-blow he knows and must swing back in return for all the ones he's received. They may be words, but they are also fists and feisty projectiles. Pablo depends on them.

Not only to fight like a man, but to keep his soul alive.

MIXED MESSAGES

———

"PABLO is right," said Odette, "when he states that *good* women can't say those *groserías*. And men can't say them in front of women. They're vulgar." Then added, "There are some women who do swear, but they are considered *bien cabronas*."

"Bien cabronas?" I asked Odette to explain. I had invited her and Adrienne, a former student of mine, over for tea. Odette was in her last year of university. I began to think that maybe young, university students could help me figure out my madre problem.

"Unfeminine, foul mouthed, *machas*, feminists. It's all the same thing," Adrienne translated from the Spanish between the lines to a Spanish that I could understand.

"Also, it is almost always thought that feminists are lesbians," Odette added.

The front door where the three of us stood opened onto a courtyard. It was filled with the quiet sounds of maids' voices chatting about their husbands while they swept the afternoon's jacaranda blooms into small purple piles.

"Say 'feminist' and the list that Adrienne gave follows with 'lesbian' at the end, like the red caboose," Odette clarified. That was the risk you'd take by using the term. You'd stir up prejudices.

But so what? Odette was giving lessons to Adrienne on how to use Mexican slang to her advantage, in a take-back-the-night or women-on-top or feminists-rock way. There was power to be gleaned from it.

I had taken a sabbatical in the mid-nineties and was staying this time in the south central part of the city, in the old, cobblestone neighborhood of San Angel-Tizapán. The buildings were two-story, not the multistoried ones of Polanco. People in this part of town lived mostly in houses that fronted onto the streets. I suppose that's why the walls were so thick, to shield out the daily clang of traffic and vendors, as well as keep the heat out in the summer or sheltered in the winter. It must also explain why there were few windows on the ground floors, and why those that were there were shaded by bougainvillea vines and jacaranda trees.

"Come in and sit down." I beckoned them inside the house.

It was always dark indoors. The only lamp that rested on the side table in the corner of the living room never had much strength. Today, however, it seemed fitting. A staged setting for a clandestine meeting of three women about to engage in a discussion of esas madres. As though we were men in a bar.

We sank down into the two plush, midnight-blue polyester couches stuffed like overfed animals. While living there I referred to them as the two sleepy hippopotamuses lounging in the mud of a murky terracotta-tiled estuary. The odd characteristic of these hippopotamuses was that they weighed absolutely nothing and would slide across the room if I sat too suddenly upon them. I was certain they were made of air. Small friends would disappear in them. Their voices emerging from the soft blue pile. They were there, somewhere. I could hear them.

"Esas madres are very strong." Odette continued. She was a descendant of fierce and powerful women, a third-generation feminist, is how she put it. Her grandmother and mother had fought for women to own property, cast a vote that counted, file for divorce, press rape charges and have the judges take the charges seriously. And Odette, she focused on the demeaning portrayal of women in society.

A friend once called her *malinchista* and what he meant was that she was like the original Malinche, an indigenous woman, Cortés' translator, whose ability to speak several languages facilitated the Spanish invasion of Mexico. Malinchistas are traitors. They have foreign interests, buy foreign products, emigrate to live in foreign lands.[1]

"Men I know use the term *malinchista* a lot, because to them it's stronger than the word traitor or *traidora*," she clarified when I asked her what her friend meant because it didn't sound so friendly to me. "He meant that I was crossing over to the other side. I wasn't being Mexican. I wasn't being like a *good Mexican woman*, that is. Well, he called me *malinchista* because of my feminism. I'm too assertive. I've got a mind of my own." Feminism, something foreign that's invading Mexico, with treacherous women translating it into practice.

She paused to take a drink.

"I decided to ignore him rather than fight over it."

Ten years after this dinner and after emerging as a professional translator, Odette sat down and wrote a thesis on English literature. Then she moved to China with her British boyfriend, now husband.

"It's not his fault, I suppose. He was taught that version of Malinche in school," someone added. Linguistically toned down for the children. But the truth is that Malinche was gifted and traded and passed from group to group, given to Cortés by her captors as an offering along with other goods. She was multilingual because of her plight, but not out of choice. She'd been enslaved since she was a young girl.

Odette, however, wasn't angered by her friend's accusation, she drew strength from it. She even liked it in a Black-Is-Beautiful kind of way, via inversion, via turning the tables on him, via becoming one of the best translators around of English into Spanish and vice versa, via wrapping herself up with the love she has of Mexico and its Spanish language while living abroad, her Mexican-British-Chinese daughter believing she's 100 percent Mexican while attending Chinese schools, speaking multiple languages, holding numerous passports.

Odette and Adrienne looked like sisters. Adrienne's strawberry blonde curls were the opposite of Odette's straight, jet black hair, but from there everything was similar. For starters, neither was the high-heeled, beauty-saloned elite of Polanco. They were both young, not much over twenty, skinny, a little over five-feet-five-inches tall, and they shared a Salvation-Army-used-clothing look that Adrienne so loved back then, where nothing quite fit and outfits were ten years out of style, which is what made them desirable.

"And there's pride among Mexican men when they use *madres*," she continued.

"Why so many, why such pride, why so strong?" I asked, then thought of the expression, *La pobreza me tira, pero el orgullo me levanta* (poverty throws me down but pride lifts me up), which I'd heard some mothers say in reference to how well their children had turned out. Against all odds, they claimed. Can this expression be used to describe how well some mothers' children toss around *esas madres*?

"Because the worst way to offend a Mexican is to say something insulting about *his* mother. His *madre*," Odette added.

Odette was Catholic, which Adrienne was not, although Odette made a point to tell me that she was no longer. Her eighteen years of Catholic schooling were in her past. "Thank God," exhaling it out of her system. And told me that it was the nuns in the school and everyone's mothers—well, not her mother, she added—who drove her crazy with their use of the Virgin as a role model for young girls. Her friends were all married or marrying and having children, and from her point of view they are acting like martyrs about it, accepting and uncritical of their roles as wives and mothers, acting like a bunch of little *Virgencitas, madres abnegadas* (self-sacrificing mothers), giving everything up for their families, for their children.

"Offend a Mexican *man*?" I asked her. "Or men *and* women?" I needed clarification. The word *mexicano*, just as the word *American* in English, could go either way.

"Men, not women."

"Some men will insult each other with a *mentada de madre*, an insult to his mother, just to pick a fight," Odette continued. "Or they will pitch these insults around as a game when they are with their *cuates*, their buddies, their fraternal twins, drinking."

While Pablo knew how to use esas madres like a man, Odette knew how to deconstruct them like a woman, into bits and pieces with a paring knife. She didn't do this like some theatrical—I mean theoretical—deconstructionist, taking the pieces apart, critiquing them and leaving them there in a puddle. Oh no. As a feminist, she took them apart and put them back together again, only different, in the way they should have been in the first place and, maybe, had been in the first place, a very long time ago. She distributed the power more equally, then gave a little more to women, as a buffer against encroachment.

"*Esas madres* are *those madres* aimed to insult someone by insulting that person's mother?" I asked. "In the U.S. I'll say, 'Fuck you' to the drivers with my windows rolled up, of course, because they might kill me. Many more individuals are armed in my country than you might think. But in Mexico, one says, if one says anything at all, 'Fuck your *mother.*' It's different. Or is it? If it is the same, it's roundabout. You've got to use a person's mother in order to get to the person." Even the English term *motherfucker* insults the guy directly, and the mother invoked is not his mother.

"Yes. It's roundabout," Odette agreed.

"But the two are related, I guess." I thought of the literal reference. I pictured a man raping another man's mother. I recalled the Puuc region in the Yucatan Peninsula of Mexico where the Maya, long before the Spaniards arrived here, carved huge penises of stone and put them on the front lawns of the ceremonial sites. Like canons, only they weren't canons, they were solid and three times the size of any canon. But they did announce unambiguously, Don't fuck with me or I'll fuck with you. The penis-as-club talk. And I thought of the Angel of Independence in the center of Reforma Boulevard, placed there to commemorate independence from Spain. Tall, erect, defiant, and victorious. Then I thought of my personal favorite, the sky-scraping column placed directly behind the massive, stone-carved madre in the Monument to the Madre in a small park, off a large boulevard in Mexico City. If I had wanted to, I could have conjured up in my mind's eye examples of phallic monuments from all over the world, because they are not limited to Mexico or to any time and place.

"In Mexico men hang out in groups all the time. Women aren't invited. In these groups they'll say all the madre insults there are in the world." Odette began to list them.

"*Te voy a partir la madre,* I'm going to break open your mother, meaning I'm going to fuck you up." Then she listed several madres with chingar, as Pablo had done.

"There are many ways to insult someone's mother, to pick a fight," she said. "They're very, very powerful."

So powerful, I learned from Odette, that even if madre herself is entirely disguised, not mentioned at all, the expressions implying those madres can incite a man to harm, even to kill. Or, more likely, bond forever with his cuates. Forever. Because while esas madres are like hot oil left on the stove to splatter and scar, they shatter the air when spoken.

"You have to be careful," Odette said. "It's not because mothers hold a high place in society. Although they do, a very high one. But *las mentadas de madre* are not about mothers as much as they are about being *macho*. It's street slang."

"Madre, no es como padre, verdad?" I asked Odette and

Adrienne. "Mother is not like father, is it?" We laughed by rolling our eyes at the reference to *padre*. Then I recalled for both of
them the time I first heard the expression *qué padre*. It was in the
studio of a Mexican artist, Laura Hernández, living and painting
in Mexico City.

"COULD YOU RETURN in three hours?" I asked the cab driver
and then rang the doorbell. Laura's head appeared through the
open window, three stories up. Next thing I knew a set of keys
came hurling down at me. With them I opened the locked gate. I
hiked up the concrete stairs on the side of the building, stepping
around the steel reinforcements that protruded in erratic fashion
from them. I was always glad for the sharp, thin rays of sun that
came through the narrow cuts made into the concrete wall of this
kind of stairwell, shortly after it was poured, around the height of
my ankles for the purpose of marking the way.

The door to her studio was propped open. Stepping through it,
I found Laura draped with yards of embroidered cottons dyed red,
purple, blue, and orange, a bouquet of blooming gladiolas. She was
holding a pot of boiling water.

"I've come to listen to you talk about your painting," I reminded
her, and accepted the fresh cup of instant coffee she handed me.
Laura's studio had few tables, no chairs, no resting places of any
kind, but the walls were covered with canvases, and there were
uncapped tubes of paint on more than one of the tables. It was
a place of action and inspiration, rather than rest and relaxation.

On one of the tables was a tall stack of finished watercolors,
each two feet long. She reached over and picked one up, dropped it
onto the bare floorboards and then circled around it. Her long skirt
inhaled and swung back and forth like a soft-sculpted pendulum,
sweeping aside the dust and animating the reclining paintings with
puffs of air. They jumped.

"The sky could have been any color," Laura explained, "but

I chose red." She swirled around the painting, her long skirt in bloom. "In life if you want the sky to be that particular red, well, tough luck. But, in painting? You can create whatever you want." Then, tossing her arms out wide, she said, "Eso es lo padre de la pintura." That is the *padre* of painting.

"Padre?" I asked. "Father?"

"Sí. Padrísimo."

"Father-*ísimo*? What does that mean?"

"Fabuloso," she sang out, dropping another picture to the floor and laughing uproariously at herself so that even her gladiolas danced and giggled.

I had a sinking feeling she was going to say that, just from the excitement of her swirls alone.

"Padre."

Like magic.

And that was the day I was introduced to padre-the-adjective for the first time.

From then on I heard it applied by a million speakers to a gazillion occasions, places, people, and things that were wonderful— your cooking, the theater, that woman's handbag, the weather, the new car, our growing friendship, the government's someday improving, the Mother's Day barbecue. *Padre, ¿no?* And it's okay to say padre in public—at lunch, on television, at gallery inaugurations, in polite company. No punches pulled if you do.

The point is that padre is above ground, well-behaved, upper class—and stands, therefore, in contrast to madre, who isn't. Which is maybe why *qué padre* is an expression that women use far more than men. You can borrow and imitate habits of the upper class in public and, by doing so, they might lift you up, but not those associated with the lower class, unless you want to make your mother mad, lose your job, confuse people.

Also padre is idiomatically far simpler than madre. "A *padrote*, or big father, is a pimp," *New York Times* journalist Alan Riding once wrote, "while something that is excellent is *muy padre*."[2] That about says it all for padre in Mexico, he concluded. Twenty-five years later, that is still true.

My take on padre that day, I said to Odette and Adrienne in recapitulating my visit to Laura's studio, was this, "Simple and unambiguous, in charge of excellence and sex."

But it left me wondering, I told them, "Why madre and not padre? What happened to madre, how did she get into this complicated situation, and, also, what keeps her there?"

ODETTE STOOD UP for a drink of water, repeating herself to make sure I understood the difference between words, actions, and *these* words. "*Las mentadas de madre* are about being macho. They're street talk."

"Her mother feels the same way about them," Adrienne added.

"When men use these madres in their expressions, it's because they feel bigger," Odette said. "*No te rajes* (Don't back down), men say." Or loosen yourself up, like a woman. Don't crack open. Like a vagina. Instead, be a *macho*.

"You have to fight to prove you are a man. It's a *machista* attitude, no? If a guy hurls one of these madres at you, and you don't respond, you're acting like a woman," Odette kept explaining. "It's like sex, women open themselves up. But men don't." Not real men. *Esas madres*. They translate, "fuck you." But if you don't fight back, they mean, "Fuck your mother—she's fucked, so you're fucked."

"And that means," she clarified, just in case I didn't fully grasp it, "you're dead."

But *good* women don't open themselves up. Girls and boys are taught this at a young age. Not their mothers. Not virgins, pure and white and heavenly like clouds, like Guadalupe, Concepción, Rosario, Luz, Dolores—or in translation, Guadalupe, Conception, Rosary, Light, and Sorrows, all common first names in Mexico. No. Not those women. Bad women open up. Like the madre down the street who opened up and then had his children . . .

"Whose children?" people whispered all the way down the block, around the corner, at the little market.

. . . one by one as she fell from grace, fucked by her children's father.

"*No te rajes.* Don't back down. You have to fight back for your honor, your manhood," Odette repeated. "They feel they have more power when they use them. They hang out in these groups and say these things."

And then I visualized the men she described, filling their vocal tracts, puffing their chests with air, extending their lips, and modifying their formant frequencies, their tongues colluding with their soft palates. A deeper voice comes from a bigger and *badder* male. That's the perception in the bush, by chimps and baboons, anyway. Now I heard it. A "*madre*" came up from their chests, over their vocal chords, into their mouths, onto their tongues, and out onto their protruding lips. And then daggers.

"It's *tu madre* who opened up. Your mother, not mine. *Yo no soy un hijo de la chingada. Yo sí tengo madre.* I'm not the son of a whore. I, yes, have a mother. Unlike you, thank you very much. And mine, she's a virgin mother. Pure as cumulus clouds at daybreak."

And I thought, madre was not only a word that had affairs with other referents, willingly or not. Madre was a weapon, the way swear words can be. Excitable. Combative. And like other fighting-word weapons, she was made of sticks and stones when she rolled off a tongue in Mexico. Depending on how madre was said, if women were present, the level of alcohol, if it were night or day. So many different ways of using her, abusing her, tossing, throwing, kicking, hurling her. To insult. Sometimes for fun like a game of cowboys and Indians. Bang, bang you're dead, where everyone has a good time. But sometimes not.

"Not me. If some guy in the street said something insulting about my mother to me, I would keep walking." Odette asserted. "I'd keep walking because I'm a pacifist. And some men would keep walking, too, just to avoid the situation. But many other men,

they would turn around and punch the guy because they wouldn't
be able to take the insult, because it would be for them a backing
down, an unlocking, an exposure."

"To admit that his own conception was not a virgin one?"

"Yeah. I suppose."

AFTER ODETTE AND Adrienne left me that afternoon, I started
to assemble into a list all the madres I had heard or found in my
correspondence and discussions with friends. My thought was once
the list was long enough, I would show them to Alberto, who
worked the front desk of a hotel nearby.

"Well?" I said to Alberto, waving a sheet of paper that reached
the floor. "Aquí están las madres." Here are the *mothers* I've
gathered.

He chuckled. He never thought I would take him up on his
offer, "Hey, whenever you need help, stop by," he had said, smiling. It was quiet at the hotel this day, and, well, why not? So I
plopped my list down on the counter, which started more or less
like this:

me vale madre, de poca madre, a toda madre,
desmadre, en toda la madre, madriza, madrazo,
me di un madrazo, le dieron un madrazo de aquellos,
mamita, mamacita, madrecita, madrina, tu madre,
peliculas de madrazo, ándale con madre,
chinga tu madre, cagate en la chingada de tu madre,
una madre, madres, bendita sea la madre,
p'a su madre, hasta la madre, y la madre,
madreador, sacar de madre a una persona,
caerle de madre a alguien, me caes de madres,
ni madre, salió de madre, madrearse, en la madre,
madrero, madrera, rayarse la madre, te voy a romper
la madre, qué madre, parece la madre del aire,

desmadrado, la madre que te parió, madre superiora,
puras madres, hecho madres, poner en tu madre,
mamitis . . .
And continued on and on.

And what did Alberto do with it? He straightened it out. He corrected my spelling, my grammar, my punctuation. He explained what I had misunderstood. That some had come from other countries. That some were used more than others. That some were totally, no matter what, off limits.

While working with him on the issue during a peaceful part of the day, I started to see just how nuanced the expressions were, and just how crisscrossed fighting words—that double as bonding words—can be. Odette and Adrienne had lifted the lid off the box. But after they left, I was inundated by a buzz of complications, zigzags, tangled up yarns swarming around me. That's when Alberto took center stage.

What I saw, with his help, were four knotted heaps into which the madres fell. There were the Ugly and Useless ones; the Fierce, Fiery, Scary, and Violent ones; the Whores; and the Sensational and Totally Awesome ones.

My list wasn't complete, Alberto pointed out, but it would never be complete because slang is organic. It grows and reproduces, dies and decomposes, and then pops up again, reincarnated into something else. Who knows how long these madres have been around.[3] Obscenities, some scholars say, are as old as religion. Others say, as old as our vocal tracts. Taking it back even further, some primatologists claim they are as old as *all* the great apes, not just us.[4]

I didn't need a complete list, I told him. I needed an impression.

He laughed. I guess he thought, given the length of my list, the impression I had was longer than most men's around here. Or women's, for that matter.

Under "Ugly and Useless" madres, and with Alberto's help, I put *me vale madre* (I don't give a damn, it's worthless, it's not important at all to me) and plain old *madres* or *qué madre* or *ay madres*, said with a dismissive voice, when mad, when life isn't going just right, when you've had some bad luck, when the motorcycle you are repairing still doesn't work. Said the way you might say, "Damn!" when things are breaking instead of mending.

Along with the *ay madres* were *está de poca madre* or *de poca madre*, literally of little mother, which means, in this case, Great. Because it is unique, singular, happened by itself, with little if any mother involved.

Then there were the little madres, the *madrecitas*, the nothing madres, the whatever madres. Like *pasame esas madres*, pass me those little-nothing-whatevers, pointing to the salt and pepper in the middle of the table, the paper clip on the corner of the desk, or that pen over there on the floor. Or you might say, I didn't believe his story, *ni madres*, not even a little. Or someone didn't complete his or her job, but handed it in anyway, and you, her co-author or boss, say, She didn't give me what I asked for, *ni madres*. Or he gave you only *madres*, nothing at all. You expected a lot more out of him than *that*. Or maybe you asked to do something, join an exclusive club, or you were too afraid to ask, thinking you didn't stand a chance, either way, you requested *puras madres*. Nada at all. And there are madres that might be used to refer to something that you don't care about, but you must do it, like your homework or the dishes or changing a diaper. I have to finish this *madre*, even though I could care less about, *y la madre*, and the mother, and so on, et cetera, et cetera, et cetera.

But then there's the "Fierce, Fiery, Scary, and even Violent" category, the big-and-watch-out bullied bunch of knotted entanglements. For example, if something has a dreadful odor, it smells of *madres*. And if it tastes bad, sounds horrendous, is a sore sight for the eyes, then it sounds, tastes, looks *madres*. Which is why when things *ir a la madre* (go to the mother), they go all to hell.

Sacar de madre a una persona (to get angry at another person) means to stick your tongue out at him or her. And, *poner en tu madre* (put it in your mother) means that someone is going to hit you or *dar en la madre* (give it to your mother) means someone is about to punch someone else. When you say, "vamos a partirle la madre" (let's split him open) or "le voy a romper la madre" (I'm going to beat that guy up), you might also be saying, Let's go kick his fucking ass, kick him where it hurts the most, in *la madre*. Where? Soft spot. Hard spot. Private spot. Or all spots. A variation of that is *ponerse en la madre* (to hit someone all over, every part of his or her body). If someone gives it to you *en la madre*, you got hit hard and all over, not just in the privates. The *madre*, the body of your mother's child. Your flesh of her flesh.

Which is why when you are *hasta la madre* (up to the mother), you have had enough to eat and are quite happy or you have had too much of that person's nonsense and are up to your ears in it. It means filled up in a good way or a bad way. And if you give it to him *en toda madre* (in the whole, total mother), it means you killed him.

In this same category I put *madriza*, a noun that refers to having the shit beaten out of you by a group of guys. And *madrazo*, which is a really hard punch, usually by only one person but might be more. You can give yourself a *madrazo,* too, by falling and banging up your knee or bumping your head or whatever you end up doing to yourself when you slip on the stairs. Violent movies are called *peliculas de madrazo*. A *madreador* is a bouncer or hired thug or even a brat in school who's always punching other kids. *Madrearse* is a verb and refers to the action of hitting, beating someone up, fucking someone over. *Vamos a madrearlo* (let's go beat the shit out of that guy). Which is why *hasta la madre* might also mean at the boiling point when you use it to say you are *really* fed up. You might even use that expression when looking back on that one mean nun or some other madre of the convent of your elementary school days. The one who struck you with a ruler to keep you in line.

In the third heap of knots I put the *puta madres*, the whore-mothers,

which are not sex workers or prostitutes, those titles would be too
gentle and wouldn't apply. Insults are strongest when users draw
upon the madres of this category.

Puta madre or la chingada madre (the whore mother, fucking
mother) is for when you are surprised, frightened, pissed off. Puta
madre is more an import from South America and not used much
in Mexico. But chingada madre, the Mexican version, yes. Chingada
madre, I can't believe I just won the lottery. Or that guy is texting
while driving and almost sideswiped me. Or puta chingada madre
because you've spent five hours putting your motorcycle back
together, and it still doesn't work. Or whatever you've done, you've
done it poorly. Or maybe someone else fucked it up, in which case
not only the chingada mother (the mother who opened up), but
your mother, la madre que te parió or la madre que te trajo al mundo
(the mother who gave birth to you; the mother who brought you
into this world), tu madre (not mine), tu chingada madre. Or tiznada
madre, if you want to temper it a bit, like friggin' instead of fuckin'.
Your shameless mother. You son of a bitch, you bastard. Today I
received a parking ticket, p'a su madre (because of your mother).
It was her fault, even though she wasn't there, had nothing to do
with it directly.

And, finally, the fourth category, the "Sensational and Totally
Awesome" madres. The mother of all mothers. The Virgin Madre
or any virgin mother. My mother, pure and heavenly, if not your
mother. And, definitely the Mother Superiora of the convent down
the street, in the next town. And if you have bad manners or no
conscience or you are just some kind of creep, then qué poca madre
tienes (what little [good] mother there is in you). You should have
more mother to be a well-mannered person, you lowlife, you idiot.

In a more mild context, if you don't have much mother in you,
then that explains why your room, your house, your life is a desmadre (a disaster, a fuckup), if we agree that the des is emphasizing
the absence of the good part. I mean the housecleaner and cook,
aka your mother, is no longer living with you, taking care of you.

Also, *desmadrado*, an adjective to mean after a wild night of alcohol, sex, and drugs, he is disheveled, even sick.

There's *a toda madre*, which is like *qué padre*, but like most other madres, it is not for polite company or formal situations or for women to use, unless those women are good friends, in the kitchen, their studios, their offices with the doors shut. Of course, women and men say it all the time, but in the right place, at the right time. If you are feeling content, without a care in the world, you feel it's your lucky day, and you are in the right company, then your life's *a toda madre*. Yesterday at the party, *me la pasé a toda madre* (I had a great mother of a time). Or you can say, Your friend, Magarita, *es a toda madre*, meaning *muy simpática*. When I heard this expression used by women, I knew they considered me a cuate and that they'd think, *Ándale con esa madre* (Go walk surrounded by a protective spirit) when I left the group.

A *madrero* or *madrera* is a man or woman, boy or girl, who just loves his or her mother. Any sex or class could use the term, because everyone loves their madre, I mean their mamá, at least in theory. A mother's love is like no other. But a person *con mamitis* (with his mother strung onto him) is a crybaby, one who can't let go of his mother, always wants his mother. Not unrelated is *mamarse* (to drink too much of a mother's milk), which means to get drunk. Or *madre de pulque*, a pulque mother, meaning a drunk, literally a person who drinks too much of the white, fermented drink that comes from the maguey cactus.

When you love others, you love them like a mother loves her children, *Yo te quiero de un amor de madre. Mucho. Mucho.* My *mamita*, my *mamacita*, my mommy. And, by the way, I'm telling you this, *bendita sea la madre que la trajo al mundo*, blessed is the mother who brought you into this world, an Arabic phrase brought by the Moors to Spain some thirteen hundred years ago and adopted into Castilian. You say it when someone does something super-duper nice. It's formal and polite to say it, even. When you really like someone, you might say, *"Me caes de madres, me caes bien,"* which is slang, but not dangerous, and translates "you fall to me from mothers, you fall well to me." That is, I like you. *Mmmmm.*

Me caes de madres, said in a tone of disgust, can mean just the opposite, however. Literally, you fall to me like a mother. I really don't like you, you're a useless nothing. For that reason, Alberto and I could have put this in the first cluster, too.

Which is why when I'm in a pickle I might prefer to invoke my mamá in warm terms to help me out in spirit if not in person, *Ay mamita*, how on earth did that happen to me, that fender bender, that situation in my office, that missed deadline? Or I might say, lovingly, "La madre," followed with an observation: my children are so wound up I can't concentrate.

And if you want that person to scram, and you're drunk or in a really bad mood, you might say "cagate en la chingada de tu madre" (go shit yourself in the rape of your mother, or go soil your fucked-up mother, the whore). Only it's a totally bad thing to say, so, I'm telling you now, Don't Say It, Ever. The idea is to insult the person's mother. You'd succeed, but can't be sure what would happen next. Because to have mother, *tener madre*, is to have honor, care about others, know shame. You would never utter mentadas de madre, if you have any mother in you. No way. Only if you have no shame, then it would be obvious that you have only a little or, come to think of it, no mother in you. That would explain why *me estás rayando la madre*, you're insulting me via my mother, another way of saying, "I've run out of patience with you." And then some.

And when everything gets out of hand, when everything has left its mother, when *todo salió de madre* (when the riverbank bursts, leaving its mother pathway to the sea), then you are in trouble.

When Alberto and I finished, I said to him, "mixed signals." Because all together these mothers are fierce and feared and adoring and virtuous and hardworking and shameful and smelly and little, insignificant nothings. And we could have doubled the list by changing the intonation of each one, which in turn changes the entire situation, from good to bad, bonding to firing and vice versa.

"But not one of them is a wallflower," I just now realized.

And he said, "¡Madre. No!" And with that he broke out laughing harder than ever.

And so did I, as I pulled out my needle and thread and strung the madres together into a barroom rosary of *Ave Madres*, along with my lists and my stepping-stones and the notes I had tucked away, while I decided where to go and what to do next.

BY THE TIME I returned to Mexico to live again, it was 2009. Both Odette and Adrienne had moved away. Armando had moved away. Pablo had found a new job and had to travel a lot. Alberto was still at the hotel, though. And I now had two soon-to-be-eight-year-old daughters with me. I had the fortune to be awarded a Fulbright fellowship, and with it came the time to dine with old friends and new ones, and, most of all, to journey with madre back inside Mexico again. I had not stopped gathering stepping-stones or making lists during my time away, but I had done so in other venues without the benefit of fresh tamales and tacos.

I chose Oaxaca over Mexico City. My girls and I had spent the summer here the year before to test it out. Oaxaca is a six-hour drive south of the country's capital, safer and more tranquil. My girls and I rented a home in a quiet, working-class neighborhood. I set up an office with an Internet connection, Skype, email, the Web. I found a school for my girls and put them in second grade. I found them an after-school babysitter, who became their best friend and mine, too. Her name was Aurora. I discovered that I could order tamales to be delivered. I did that. I made fresh margaritas with tiny, perfectly rounded limes I bought by the kilo in the market right up the street and served them to friends on our roof, which had an eastern view and when timed just right we could toast each other and our madres and padres while the moon rose. On holidays my Mexico City friends visited. Once a month, between holidays, my daughters and I visited them. And in the middle of all the comings and goings I met a whole new batch of friends and acquaintances, libraries, archives, newspapers, and museums.

I went to work, starting with my list of madres that Alberto had helped me define and organize.

I first called Jane Bussey, the journalist. She, too, had moved away, after fifteen years of living in Mexico, but I found her on assignment in Mexico City and we met for dinner. She said exactly what Odette had said, It's not about mothers so much as it is about men and the disdain men have for their mothers. She had seen over the years plenty of examples of the "matriarchy inside Mexican homes," a contrast to the patriarchy outside them. These mother insults are about power and control over women who exercise power and control over their children at home. The sons, especially, don't like it.

"Matriarchy?"

I Skyped Armando. He agreed, but added, with the perspective of a son, it's also about mothers. "Yes, there is a matriarchy and men feel emasculated by it," is how he put it. "However, it's also about the dark side of the *abnegada*, self-effacing, self-sacrificing woman, you hear about but never meet. I have male friends who are in therapy trying to recover from their mothers, after being held hostage their whole youth by what they call the 'cult of the Mexican mother,' the kind you see in the Mexican soap operas, manipulative and self-serving."

"A *mother* cult?" I asked but knew from experience that a person only has to witness Mother's Day here to understand the pedestal onto which mothers are placed. Bigger than Independence Day.[5] For decades, scholars have been trying to define this mother cult. No one denies its existence, but What, When, Where, Why? Back in the 1970s, anthropologist Evelyn Stevens called it *marianismo* (the emulation of the Virgin Mary), linked it to the Church, and placed its origins in the colonial period, before Mexico's Independence from Spain in 1810 and the rise of the secular state. It was a small article that became a big controversy.[6]

The problem was that as court documents, census reports, letters, and literature from postcolonial nineteenth-century Mexico City indicate, and as historian Sylvia Marina Arrom discovered while reading boxes and books of them, there was no secular mother cult prior to the nineteenth century, inspired by Church doctrine or not. Until then the Church tended to see everyday mothers and fathers equally as parents, while colonial society considered mothers inferior to fathers. They were lacking in education and virtue and in need of protection and discipline. When they were widowed, their children were often removed from them because of their presumed incompetence as a parent.[7]

So what happened?

According to Arrom, around the 1850s the Liberals, the political party in power and well known for being anti-Church, were nervous about women's growing participation in the public sphere. Establishing motherhood as venerable and the home as sanctified— as the Victorian British had done with great success—would give women a sphere of their own where they could be boss. Also, it would keep them off the streets and out of the workplace where they had begun to compete with men for jobs.

Under their watch, everyday motherhood became an exalted *madre*-hood. And hence forward. The twentieth-century Revolutionaries who succeeded them took the idea and ran with it, adding in 1922 a ritual, Mother's Day, and in 1949, a shrine, the *Monumento a la Madre*, where the monumental mother and child stands above the words, "To the woman who loved us before even meeting us," and is flanked on one side by a man writing and on the other by a woman holding an ear of corn, a symbol of fertility and sustenance. Mexican cinema, literature, newspapers, and even the Church, after a while, helped make it into a cult.

Now I'm wondering, more than 150 years after the Liberals set up house, Were the seeds of my madre list sown inside this

nineteenth-century, anticlerical, holy matrix of Liberal machinations and madre-superior discourse? Because, while swearing works best at forcing another's blood pressure to go way up
when sacred symbols on pedestals—held by those in earshot—are
inverted, you need the sacred symbols to start with. Which is why,
by the way, if you ever find yourself on a pedestal, you need to
beware. Because the first heads to be toppled in a Revolution are
those on pedestals.

I turned to Aurora, our new babysitter. In fact, I started to
ask her questions almost before she knew my name or why she'd
been hired. I showed her the list. For the nine months we lived
in Oaxaca, I talked to Aurora more than I talked to anyone. I
considered her the perfect consultant because she was young and
educated and in charge of her life, saving her money for a five-year
nursing program at the University. She'd like to have a family.
Maybe, someday, be married. But not just then.

At first I felt bad about my barrage of questions. After all, Aurora
was a sitting duck, especially at lunchtime, when she and I sat
together, my girls having abandoned the table as soon as possible
to swing in the hammocks on the porch. But I came to believe
she liked the topic because she began to return from her weekends
away with data in hand.

"If a matriarchy inside the house is responsible for the plethora
of madre insults, then why hasn't the patriarchy outside the house
engendered padre insults?" Seemed a reasonable enough question.
But try as I might, I was unable to find even one *me vale padre*
anywhere.

"Maybe it's because mothers are the main disciplinarians here,"
was one of her early responses. She had a daughter's perspective.
And in many cases fathers weren't around. *Out of sight, if not out
of mind*, might be the paraphrased answer to my question. Or if
around, they were not the ones to discipline as much as to play
with their children, like many fathers most places in the world.
"The mother is in charge of what goes on inside a house as far as

offspring go, anyway. She is the one who sees to it that children have social skills, learn good manners, dress well, comb their hair, brush their teeth, pick up, help out." That's how she described her own mother.

When Judith, the housekeeper and a mother of two boys, came on Mondays to check on the house's vital signs, the water pump, the gas, the cistern, I showed her the list, and asked, "Can you help me make sense of this?"

"Beware," is what she said and slapped the back of her hand down onto the palm of the other with such force I straightened my posture and stood at attention. Her two boys were now grown up. One had finished college and had a good job, the other had two more years of culinary school to go and had begun to work as a chef. He'd already become famous for his chocolate truffles. While her husband had been around the whole time, he'd never been in charge. She had been. And, by the way, she still was.

The way she smacked her hands together I thought of the word *madrazo*, which I didn't mention.

I asked Alejandro, Judith's husband. He agreed with Judith, shaking his head in a way that bespoke fear. He put in a word for her as someone who would have no problem motivating my girls to do their homework—and on time. I considered it, as I was getting nowhere with them on that issue.

I thought of Judith, while reading comparative child psychology reports on parenting in Mexico and in the United States because the authors claimed that mothers in contemporary Mexico were, without a doubt, in charge of the house. And, yes, often with a heavy hand. They found this to be true up and down the class ladder.[8] Nannies, helping with the housework, didn't seem to make a difference. Reading these reports made me think, also, of my close Mexican friends Claudia, Magali, Elena, Teresa, Laura, along with Aurora's mother, all of whom were left out of those studies, surely, because they are all the biggest pushovers you'll ever meet, sparing the rod to spoil their kids.

I talked with Aurora and Judith about anthropologists who had studied up the class ladder, like Larissa Lomnitz, and those who had studied down the class ladder, like Matthew Gutmann, in their respective books on upper-class and lower-middle-class families in Mexico City, and how they had both found that mothers were in charge of making sure their children turned out all right. This involved nothing short of directing the trains in the house to run on time and the kids to board and disembark on schedule. And fathers? They were available for playing and having fun or running the business outside the house.[9]

"Qué padre," we said in concert. By that we meant, How cool would that be to assume your role as a parent is above the dishes and the laundry and the homework and the getting everyone out the door each morning, fed, and to bed each night?

The problem is, you can't keep the trains running on time by coming home on occasion to play with the kids. And we pointed to *desmadre* and *qué poca madre tienes* on my list because that's what happens when there is no mother or grandmother around in Mexico. Things fall apart.

Aurora told me about her father. He began his third family when she was born, and he stayed with her mother for five years before he left to start a fourth family. He had a bad heart and died young, not yet fifty years old. He never sent any money, anyway, but he called from time to time, and the day before his fatal heart attack he had promised to pick up Aurora and her brother and take them to the beach. He so rarely called, so their visit with him was going to be extra special. They would spend the weekend together, build sand castles, swim in the waves of a sandy cove on the Oaxacan coast, eat ice cream.

Qué padre, we said again, but in tears. Because mixed messages can also mean mixed up. Then I began to see why men use the madre insults far more than women, and why women use qué padre far more than men. To each group, there was power to be gained. One by disassociation and provocation, the other by association. But there was no escaping notice that the former tears apart to produce its power, while the latter builds upon it.

And that's around the time when Antonio, a journalist in Mexico City, who has lived there all his life, made a suggestion, You have to read Octavio Paz's "Los hijos de La Malinche," to understand anything at all about those madres.

I had grown up reading Paz. I had taught his books in my classes. I had gone to his seventy-fifth birthday party at the Palace of Fine Arts in Mexico City. Paz, a Nobel laureate, was the most influential Mexican essayist, poet, and intellectual of his day, beginning with the 1950 publication of his *Labyrinth of Solitude*, where his famous essay on Malinche appears.

Paz's nineteenth-century grandfather, Ireneo, had cast Malinche as a traitor in two of his novels.[10] But Octavio saw Malinche as far more than malinchista. She was Mexico's personal Eve, synonymous with—and here's the twist on the biblical version—*La Chingada*. As Mexico's First Mother of a mestizo nation, she disgraced her people by opening up to the raping Spaniard, Cortés, and by bearing his son. Paz, the grandson, did not spend much time talking about Cortés as the father of Mexicans, as their Adam. He stayed focused on the repercussions of Malinche's indulgence.

"Los hijos de La Malinche" is a weighty, twentieth-century narrative. Weighty because there is no salvation. No way to forgive this original sin of Malinche that is repeated in the birth of every Mexican since—all children born in Mexico are children of La Chingada. No secular baptism of any kind to wash away her sin, which hangs heavy on her children, like an albatross and throughout the generations forever.

What was the information in that narrative that had Antonio thinking I'd find answers to my madre questions there? Was the pathos of this story of Malinche, as told this way, a clue?

Alberto at the hotel had explained that chinga tu madre goes like this: Fuck your mother, meaning, *She's fucked, so you're fucked.*

Because if your mother is fucked, and you are her child, there goes your reputation inside the blood of her shame seeping from under the door of your house and running down the street for everyone to see.

Which is why what came to my mind right now was not Malinche but the stories of honor and shame that anthropologists have gathered from towns around the Mediterranean and that were brought here by the Spaniards way back when. These stories of sexually passive and shameful women—and, sometimes, men—stigmatize. Stigma can really limit a person's power—on purpose.[11] So that narratives of good mothers, those planted in the nineteenth century, found themselves accompanied by those of bad mothers. And Malinche, who had practically been seen as the Virgin incarnate by the Spaniards—her name was a transformation of the Spanish María into Nahuatl, after all—came to play the Betrayer in the nineteenth century and then the full-fledged *Chingada* in the twentienth.[12]

I asked Judith, "What do you think of Octavio Paz's narrative on La Malinche?" I was curious, as no one in Oaxaca ever recommended I read Paz, only friends and acquaintances in Mexico City.

"I know the expression, *Somos hijos de la Chingada*," she told me. "I've heard of La Malinche. But I don't feel like a 'son of the violated mother.' And, no, I have never heard of Octavio Paz or his book. Reading is for lazy people."

I laughed so hard I almost cried. Because master narratives are *master* narratives, written by masters not mistresses. That doesn't disqualify them. Only to say that it can be difficult to make sense of them sometimes if you are not a master yourself. Who are these guys talking about? Then I thought, Maybe the translation of *hijos* into "sons" rather than "children," whether in English or Spanish, was the accurate choice. It's more a guy problem. That's what Odette, Jane, and Armando had said. The *hijas* (daughters) I've met down here don't seem to have this knotted up relationship with their mothers.

ONE EVENING NOT long ago, I sat on the terrace of our rental house in Oaxaca. To my right was a stack of dictionaries, on my lap was the list of madres and pile of notes, on the table in front of me was my computer. It was a typical picture, one that my daughters just photographed for posterity. Great. I looked like a wreck. I hadn't had a haircut in months. Forget about makeup. My clothes? The same ones from yesterday, not to mention the day before. And just as I went off thinking I really needed an overhaul, a *cohete* (a really loud firecracker, like a bomb) went off somewhere in our neighborhood. Or maybe it was an AK-47. "Holy shit. What was that?" I shouted, standing up and sending the *madres* scattering.

Just then I had a realization. In my determination to understand the recipe for making esas madres into projectiles with piercing effects of various kinds, I'd left out a basic ingredient: just how good it can feel to swear.

Maybe you don't know what I'm talking about. So, you'll have to take my word for it.

Because whether one curses up a storm or uses only one word once in a blue moon, it is not only the language processing centers in the left side of the brain that are firing away as you exclaim yourself, but your basal ganglia *and* limbic system as well. The basal ganglia is where production of these profanities occurs and where impulse control and aspects of motor functions, habit formations, and learning are found inside a complex set of nuclei deep within the brain. *And* the limbic system, especially the amygdala, is where affective perception of these fiery words occurs, where long-term memory, behavior, and emotion are located and where the origin of our fight-or-flight chemical production transpires also deep within the brain. Two very, *very* old parts of our brains are at work.[13]

Here's the point: while cursing causes the pulse to rise, the hairs to bristle on those within earshot, it is equally true that swearing works to relax, to relieve tension for those uttering the coarse language, when alone or among friends. In fact, to Timothy

Jay, author of *Why We Curse*, swearing is "a form of anger management" that is highly underrated.[14] Now that the cohete next door scared the you-know-what out of me, I totally agreed. My split-second instinct was to find the guy who'd set it off and give him one heck of a madrazo. But, then, after swearing, I sat back down instead and broke out laughing with Aurora and my girls.

With that summation, I recalled Pablo writing under the midnight oil. Each time he cast into the night air another madre, to be read by me at the end of an Internet connection, he shed a wee little bit of the weight he associated with bad, corrupt politics that hung heavy in his weary mind.

FOOD FIGHT

A YEAR after Odette and Adrienne came for tea, they
returned for dinner. They brought their close friends,
Poppy, another American their age and a former student of mine;
Luis, David, and Tony, Mexican students in their early twenties
and late teens. Artists and food types, to whom they assured my
harmlessness.

She's an anthropologist who'd heard it all.

(And understood not a thing.)

Say what you will.

I welcomed them in, served them a drink, and offered them
a seat on the hippopotamuses. After some cheese and crackers,
drinks, and introductions they turned to teaching me a lesson
about sex in Mexico and how to understand that a single word
phrase can have at least two meanings, depending on the context,
tone of voice, and delivery, and how to catch them in your mitt
and throw them back. It was to help me understand madre more,
even though she played no role in these games.

"*Buenas noches,* little mama. Good evening, *mamacita.*" David and
his friend Luis began to explain the distinction to me in Spanish.
"It depends how you say it and to whom if it is a *piropo* or an *albur.*"

"A woman is walking by. You've never met her. She's beautiful. So you, a man, say, 'Buenas noches.' Perhaps add, 'Ay, qué linda,' how very pretty. Maybe 'mamacita.' Those are *piropos*."[1]

Compliments, flattery, *echado por la calle* (thrown at her), while walking down the street. Soft whispers, like rose petals tossed out in front of her, or maybe like a bowling ball rolled at her, to knock her down. I wasn't sure. I was hoping that David and Luis, along with the others who came with Odette that evening, would help me understand what was what and which was which.

David and Luis continued.

"If you say, 'Qué buena está la noche' and/or 'Ay, qué buena' and mean more than 'the night is lovely' and 'how nice,' then it is an *albur*. She's lookin' good, the night is. That's an *albur*, not a *piropo*, because *albures* always have double meanings, and the second one is always sexual."

Pay attention. Because focusing on the piropo is like focusing on the decoy instead of the duck.

"It's also sexist," Odette tolled. Odette, who was among some of her closest friends this dinner, played the role of the devil's advocate, the young feminist, and this gave more shape to the evening. She agreed with some on piropos, but drew the line on albures. Odette felt it was okay to have her body complimented by men on the street, but most compliments, she believed, were sexist.

Piropos or albures, they all seemed sexist to me back then. Which is why learning Spanish in the 1980s was a challenge for me because I was also a feminist of a certain sort, mostly the irreproachable sort, pissed off, with only a wee drop of humor in me. As I grew older, I gained a better hold on my life. I knew what I had to do, I started to keep the pen I hold in my hand dripping with fresh ink. And with that my laughter returned, like a long lost friend.

Also back then, practically speaking, I was younger and so more an object of desire to men. Being over-the-hill has its advantages.

But in Ohio and New England, where I grew up, comments and whistles that came from men I'd never met were limited to construction sites, passing cars with a load of fraternity boys, and an occasional inebriated married man.

In Mexico it was different. More often than not these comments came frequently, and by a man operating all by himself. In a business suit. In overalls. I'm not sure I ever walked down the street in Mexico without someone reaching out to touch my hair or say "Pretty one, will you marry me?" or something of the sort. It made me uncomfortable. I'd cross the street if I saw a man coming along in the opposite direction—even at high noon—or standing along the wall looking like he had nothing better to do. I stayed clear of the curb, too, because there were drivers who would reach out their windows, honk their horns. My peripheral vision was on guard, all times of day.

Luis met Odette halfway. "Buenas noches could be a piropo even with the second meaning, but it's a low one. And these are sometimes said to be piropos because the woman does not respond."

"Well we do not know if she does or not," Odette said.

"When a man goes into the street and says something to a woman that has a double meaning and it is directed at you, you won't want to respond."

Keep walking. Look directly ahead, down, up, over. Just not, whatever you do, at him.

"Because some man is making an albur about you," David and Luis clarified.

"They're sexist," Odette repeated herself. [2]

"They refer to sex," David emphasized.

"But not in the make love sense. Rather, in the chingar sense, to fuck someone, the fucker being the winner and the fucked, the loser," Odette, fleshed out the explanation, "which is why albures are also machista." Odette spoke like her mother, the way she peppered her speech with these words and others like *pinche* and *pendejo*, damn and asshole, so much. Very Mexican words, which a

Peruvian friend of mine used to love to say by aspirating the *p*'s as did Liza Dolittle in *My Fair Lady* the *h*'s for Hartford, Harrington, and Hampshire. They were more explosive that way.

Not compliments by men but male complements, like the way burrs complement your pant legs when you walk through the woods.

The albur is not just a sexual joke, or a way to make a joke, a *picardía* or a *doble sentido* or a pun type of joking. It's a game. Your turn, my turn. There are winners and losers. And it plays with the subconscious more than the conscious, the id more than the ego. The albur comes from the Arabic word, *al-bur*, the root of which means uncultivated, a fallow field, an uneducated, weed-filled mind that goes off in all directions and produces little fruit to eat, not enough to store for the winter.[3] But in the chaos it produces, there's potential—if you're savvy enough to notice.

Mexican men are geniuses at making albures. Not all but most. So are some women. But they're of a man's world. There's a pecking order. And women on occasion peck away at others to create their place in line. Sometimes it's to tease or flirt, they're young and want to play with the boys. But also, just like the men, they'll do it to insult, especially other women.

"Would everyone like an enchilada?" I interrupted. I served, before its time, Chinese-Mexican fusion, where I put black gooey *huitlacoche*, a mushroom delicacy, inside the translucent skins of Chinese pasta and floated them on a mango sauce with avocado garnish. A huitlacoche egg roll at sea.

"Dinner is ready. Please, sit down."

"*Salud.*"

We reached into the center of the table with our drinks. "To our health. To your health." And continued to talk more about the albur tongue twister.

David chimed in. "Ever since you are a child, you learn how to *alburear*. No matter what class. Some more than others, but almost all men know how to make albures." Men and boys in taxi cabs, in bars, on the street, at school, in the locker rooms, dining rooms, parlors. Where men congregate, if appropriate, if from the same class, if someone breaks the ice, if the other wants to engage, if Mexican. *Somos mexicanos.* Not "as," the feminine, but "os," the masculine. *Mexican-OS.* Men. *Hombres de verdad* (Real men). On top. Masculine.

"Women don't alburean. It's something men do. It isn't proper," he added.

"Some women do," Odette countered, "that's changing. That's been changing." Adrienne and Poppy sat on either side of her. They'd come along to learn more Spanish and more about how to alburear. Odette had plenty of girlfriends who could put any man to shame albureando, but they couldn't make it to dinner. "They are called *albureras*," she said.

"But it's not proper."

"Well," she pealed, "women have not traditionally *alburean* because they don't have a *pajarito,* so they automatically are *chingada,* fucked," while putting her tongue in her cheek. She's sort of like Pablo in that way. Because the albur almost always has to do with who does you-know-what to whom. She continued, its "Not proper to say 'penis,' not for a mother, not sister or daughter, not for any woman who models herself after the *Virgen Santa.* It's a *pajarito,* a little bird." The nuns told her this in school.

"A wee wee, a little weiner. Penis, in the diminuitive," Adrienne translated, laughing.

"Penis in the diminuitive?"

"You can also say *paloma,* a dove," someone added.

"So maybe any bird."

"Because of the beak?"

"Just don't say the actual word. Puh-lease," Odette said. She loved sarcasm, and to make fun of the nuns and the way they talked about body parts. They could never actually say the words that were in the dictionary or call a body part by its anatomical name.

"Poppy and Adrienne are different," David quickly noted. "I'm teaching them how to alburear, but it's not typical for women to learn, although some do, especially the younger ones. Not my mother, for example. Odette already knows a lot about it, but that's because of her mother who raised her as a feminist and to say as she pleased." As a female, Odette didn't learn to alburear as easily as David, Tony, and Luis, her male buddies. But determined, she and the new crop of upper-middle-class feminists were all learning how to do it, part of breaking out of their Catholic school days.

"Just like before there were only male rappers, now there are female rappers," Adrienne said.

"At first," Odette added, "being a woman and learning how to alburear was hard because I couldn't understand what the boys were saying. Their jokes were so regional. In addition, they had some words that they had made up and used only among themselves." The inside jokes of lovers, sisters, brothers, and families or other in-jokes that form part of the daily language of a tightly knit group can get lost in translation, lose their punch if you have to explain them. Not only were the jokes largely male, but in Odette's case, the *chilangismos* (expressions from Mexico City) that composed them were even harder to grasp than all the gendered nuances within them. Odette, like Adrienne, was not from D.F., but from Orizaba, a city in Veracruz, and had recently moved here.

"For me," Adrienne said, "learning how to alburear gave me a feeling of belonging. Like you feel when you're able to deliver the perfect punch line. Or when you know the call-and-response phrases in a complicated chant. Or, this may sound odd, but it's like the way you feel when you know what to say at a Catholic Church service." Totally in the know, on key, in synch, a member of the club.

Then right there at my dinner party I found myself caught inside one of these things.

"Están muy chicos," someone said. "They are very small"— referring to the small size of the egg rolls.

"Pasame el plato grande" (pass me the large plate), David

responded. *Plato,* the word for plate in Spanish is an albur because it can mean penis, in case you didn't know. What with a *plato* being round and flat, you might have missed that association. Not to mention that the word or reference was entirely outside the conversation, as there were no large plates to pass. But for Luis and Tony it was a bone. David was throwing an *albur* at them. For others at the table it might have been a derailment, a non sequitur, but it wasn't for *these* others. For women generally, it would have been left unacknowledged, if even recognized, because for proper women to engage in such banter is a no-no. Although it wasn't for *these* women, the ones who came to dinner.

On the contrary.

"¿Como?" Luis hit it back to David with his tongue. Luis could follow David *and* lead him on. "Como" is a homonym that can translate into What or How or I'll eat it, context dependent. *¿Como?* if you are asking, "How might I pass it to you? Or *¿Como?* if you need someone to repeat what she or he has just said because you didn't hear it. Or *¿Como?* if you are using the first-person singular of the verb *comer,* to eat—"May I eat now?" Luis meant all of the above, of course.

"Sientate. Te ves cansado" (Sit down, you look tired). David was quick. Sit down on my *plato grande.*

Luis explained, "Sometimes you are talking about nothing in particular, you look at what's on the table, then you draw upon the contents, in this case, the avocados, egg rolls, mangoes, and plates, to enter into the albur."

Food is a common way to start an albur session among guys, especially when there is no woman present.

"Avocados, eggs, melons, lemons, limes, peanuts, *tejocotes,* all are testicles," Tony began to list all the foods he knew that were either men or women or parts of them.

"You make them up on the spot," David added. "You are talking, and you say something that could have another meaning and you or the other person bridge it to something sexual. With your imagination you make an albur. Cucumbers turn into penises, mangos into breasts, papayas into vaginas."

So albures are composed of puns, and puns are a kind of bilingualism. One may be fluent in Spanish, but inside an albur, every word you thought you knew has another meaning, not listed in the dictionary. You can talk and talk and talk about sex and never mention vagina and penis because, well, how vulgar of you. People will hear you. You'll be found out. They'll look down on you. It's low class to talk that way. But in an albur, no one will know what you are saying—except those who know. And they are most likely your friends. Or Mexicans, anyway. Because Mexicans, that is Mexican men, who are worth their chili pepper are bilingual in that way.

"It happens inside a normal conversation."

You either see it—I mean hear it—or you don't. A tacit agreement to step into the looking glass for a minute or two with another person, using another language.

"Cucumbers, bananas, sweet potatoes, carrots, corn-on-the-cob, sausage," Tony continued with his list. "These all mean penis."

As forks, spoons, and knives plunged into the huitlacoche egg rolls, black fungus oozed out into the mango, a viscous evening cloud into a pulpy sunset.

"There's no methodology, per se," David and Tony explained, "except albures must have rhythm and rhyme."

And synonyms and homonyms, prefixes and affixes, metaphors and metonyms, food and clothing, roots and branches, trunks and canopy.

"And speed," David added.

Be quick with your words and actions. Alburear is a game of wit like arm wrestling, a poetic entanglement, the Mexican tango.

And, then, a curve ball.

Because the albur is not just any sexual joke. It's not like jokes you hear in Argentina or Colombia or Puerto Rico or Cuba or anywhere else in the world, because of course they are everywhere.

Even in the Dominican Republic, where the word "albur" translates the same as in Mexico, a sexual joke, it's not the same as in Mexico.[4] Similar, but different.

Same with the Dozens, a verbal-sparring game associated with African Americans in Philadelphia and other U.S. cities back in the middle of the last century. Because the Mexican albur, like the Dozens, is a duel. It's a contest, a fight, a battle, a metaphorical gunfight. It's real combat. Even when the fire is friendly. And you don't want to lose. Even the victor doesn't want you to lose because the pleasure of winning is mixed with the victor's resentment toward the vanquished. However, Mexican albures are also different from the Dozens because they all but forbid mentioning one's mother. The Dozens included her.[5]

"Tejocote. Te cojo. Cojote," fell from Luis' mouth. It was a swift rearrangement of the Mexican hawthorn's round yellow, plum-size fruit, *tejocote*, pronounced taehocotae, into *te cojo* and *cojote*, two ways of saying I'm going to fuck you. *Cojer*, to take or to pick, means in Mexico to take sexually. You never *coge* a taxi in Mexico or a mango from a tree as you might elsewhere in Latin America, unless you are inside an albur.

"Also trumpets, cornets, trombones, tubas," Luis joined Tony's production of penises.

"Albures fall on you," Luis explained.

They also drop on you, are tossed, thrown, thrust, swung at you. Piropos are rose petals. Albures the bowling balls. They are metaphors men live *by* and women live *with*, even the one's learning to do it. The sensibility, oh-so-very male. Sometimes albures are rings in a juggling act, at other times a fast serve in a game of tennis, and still others, switchblades in a fight.

It depends who is in the game. Friends alburean for fun, acquaintances to bond or fight, others to really, truly vanquish a foe.

"But with friends it's fun," Adrienne said. "Having the chance to learn how to alburear, even a little, is deliciously satisfying." Not to vanquish her foe, she said, but to be a member of a club, to be included because she knew what was happening and not have the wool pulled over her eyes and at her expense.

SOME YEARS AFTER this dinner, while earning her doctorate, Adrienne spent time with gangs in Honduras who had spent time in Mexico.[6] Her ability to alburear like a Mexican man came in handy, a non-Mexican woman speaking Mexican-man talk. The gang members, who had learned the talk while in exile, liked that about her. Of course she spoke differently, educated and upper class, when interviewing members of the Honduran government. As did her Honduran gang friends when in front of authorities, like the police. Linguists call this code switching. But people on the ground? They call it staying alive.

"Once Tony taught me," Adrienne illustrated a few points for me, "that when he routinely said 'Okey, te lo lavas' to his cuates as his particular way of saying 'See you later,' it translated 'Okay, go wash yourself,' but implied 'Go wash your anus.' And the response would be, 'Te guardo el agua' (I'll save you the water), and sometimes it went further, 'para que hagas gárgaras con ello' (so that you can gargle with it). We had a few other cued word games like that." And they were albures that were outside the sexist category and not unlike the innocent, See you later alligator, In a while crocodile, but they were not for children.

"Pens, pencils, paintbrushes, fingers, skinny ones. But, also, guns, pistols, rifles, machetes, sticks, clubs. Grenades. Weapons of all types," Tony and Luis added more synonyms to their list.

"And when they fall on you, you have to swing back," David warned.

The rings, the ball, the switchblade. Back and forth, in and out, until one person wins by saying the last line, the punch.

"You have to defend yourself against losing and exposing yourself. You have to prove you are a man, not a woman."

That's the male sensibility part.

"Chilies, crabs, lobsters," Tony tried to remember all the foods that pinch, prick, and wound.

"And then it's over," Luis said.

"Of course, if you lose in an albur, you can still have the last word by saying, 'Me la ganas pero al burro se la mamas,'" David retorted. "You beat me, but now you'll have to suck the *burro*, the burro, the small donkey."

"It's homosexual," Odette tolled again. "Because men are traditionally the ones who engage in putting albures together, they end up fucking each other."

"No. It all depends who's on top."

"For semen there is milk, yogurt, juice, cream, *jocoque* (a drink made from soured milk), coconut milk, toothpaste," Tony continued.

"Albures are about being a man," Luis and David insisted. "It all depends who loses, whose on the bottom, who opens up."

When they are young, boys learn to talk sex by climbing into an albur. First one, then the other. First the talk, and the magazines of naked women their fathers give them. The doing they learn in other ways, or maybe not. You'll have to ask their wives and their lovers.

"Well, albures are about rape, about threatening violent sex with your opponent," Odette countered.

"Albures are also about sisters and mothers and grandmothers, and the woman passing by, not just about other men," Luis added.

Because they are about the forbidden, too. They are especially about the forbidden.

"Frijoles, beans, peanuts, coffee, compost, chocolate," Tony started to list words for anus and excrement.

I started to think about my nephews. How at three, four, five, eight, fourteen, sixteen years of age, they laughed hysterically at, well, burping, vomiting, farting. The body all by itself, uncultivated, on its own. Full of wild weeds.

"Udders, chicken breasts, melons, mangos, *chicharrón* (fried pork fat), headlights, all words for breasts," Tony now focused on women.

"But, more than anything, about sisters because one feels a certain amount of respect toward a mother," David added.

"But not toward the sister?"

"Well, no. Lots of albures joke about sisters, but not about mothers."

"No. No. The sister is sort of, although not really, okay. But the mother is really, really forbidden in albures."

Odette added, "Shhhhhh. Remember? Too close to the Virgin Mother. My mother. Your mother. And now all my friends who are mothers, the *virgencitas* or, I mean, *Virgencitas* who went to school with me."

"Papaya, just about any fruit cut open, but especially the papaya. Also cognac, *molcajete* (a mortar for grinding salsa)," Tony turned to listing substitutes for vagina.

"Oiga compa,' como está su hermana" (Listen my friend, how is your sister)? someone began to recite from memory. "I mean how *is* she?" Meaning, Is she *buena*? Is she good, is she voluptuous?

"No tengo hechas" (I don't have a sister), someone responded, and then the game began.

"Las hacemos, no hay problema" (We can make 'em, no problem. We can make some sisters for you). Me and *your mother*, that is.

"Hagame un favor, paseme mi chaqueta" (Do me a favor, hand me my jacket), which is an inside way of saying, "Jerk me off."

"Le voy a hacer un favor pero de nueve meses" (I'll do you a favor, alright, but it will take nine months), meaning I'll have an affair with your mother, which is implied, never mentioned directly, and she'll make some sisters for you once she gets pregnant.

"It is not easy to learn how to alburear. You have to practice to be good at it," David said. "But a guy who cannot alburear is a *pendejo*, a fool, a simpleton, less than manly."

"The *molcajete* and the *tejolote*, the mortar and pestle, make the most flavorful tomato and chili salsa," Tony was now onto ways to describe sexual intercourse. He started out gently not sure of how far he could go in front of the older folks in the room. Me, that is. Then he added, "*Echar, pegar, matar*, thrusting, causing harm, killing. *El palo, la pistola*, with sticks, clubs, and guns. Striking blows, hurling the stick."

Years after this dinner, working in a kitchen at a country club in Miami, Tony's jokes with his Cuban co-workers fell flat. They didn't see what he saw when he looked at a plate, although they did share something with papayas, a word so incendiary in Cuban slang that Cubans altered the name of the fruit altogether. And so he spent his cooking days dreaming of Mexico's pyramidal stacks of chilies and mangos in the marketplace. Although he didn't, and to this day doesn't, much miss Mexico beyond the food and the jokes. He has a family now in Florida, a wife, a daughter he adores heart and soul, and will talk about for hours if you let him. And now, after cooking mostly Mexican food all these years, he's a chef at an Asian fusion restaurant, maybe serving huitlacoche egg rolls.

But Tony knows that as far as his humor goes, albures are about being Mexican, part of a Mexican man's national identity. That's what a lot of Mexican men say, ones with a lot of authority, going right back to Octavio Paz, Armando Jiménez, later Carlos Monsiváis, and now the next generation, younger people like Victor Hernández, at his website. And bloggers of all sorts.[7] Albures, they have all said one way or another, are about being Mexican.

Do women think this?

Does everyone think this?

Oh you can psychoanalyze albures and talk about a latent homosexuality or see them as exhibiting an active anxiety that men have about their manhood. Just how big or small or manly is it? You can see sexual jokes psychologically as lifting sexual inhibitions like a good shot of tequila. Or anthropologically, sexual jokes as liminal and on the margins, in which inversions and suspensions of the social order occur, like they do during Mardi Gras or Carnival. Or attacking the social order, lightening the social order, exaggerating the social order. Or heterosexual masculinity's preoccupation with homosexuality or homosexual masculinity's preoccupation with heterosexuality. And a million other academic ways of picking apart, figuring it out, looking for subaltern agency, for uncalled-for hegemony. And then you can see the jokes as harassment, but you have to move away from looking at the joker to noticing the joked upon.[8]

On first, second, and third thought, I bet they engage in all of those actions, and even all at once, simultaneously.

But to Odette, it's none of the above. "They are only words." That's what she told her cuates at dinner. She wanted to say women can rap, too, and with or without the Fuck You. As far as she was concerned, her use of them was a way to verbally finesse and critique the pistols, pencils, pens, and paintbrushes, in other words, the itsy-bitsy pajaritos that are out there in the population.

"Or is it a sign of compliance, when a woman alburea?" I had to ask. It was my turn to play the devil's advocate. Was it participation based on a fuck-you/you're-fucked approach, a totally phallocentric kind of participation?

"I stay away from the sexist albures," Adrienne said, and then she went on to say that she sticks to the ones that burp and fart. Otherwise women rappers are like male rappers and, well, for them it's all about their *pajaritos* and *palomas*, their sticks and stones, their clubs and guns. About, if we are going to be analytical about it, their coming home big when they're feeling small.

Years after this dinner Tony, Odette, Adrienne, and I have kept in touch by way of email: Tony in Miami, Adrienne in Cairo, Odette in Beijing. Not long ago, I sent Adrienne a draft of this chapter, which triggered her rethinking.

"When I joke with Tony about saving my bathwater for him, I don't feel like I'm engaging in sexist behavior. I'm just one-upping him in an immature but fun game. And one-upping him in a way that he taught me to do. He gets a lot of satisfaction when I get him back, and laughs heartily if I come up with a new, yuckier addition.

If we were albureando about something specifically offensive to women, I would think differently. But when Mexican women alburean, they can get men back at that game, too. Albeit still relying on some of the tools of the patriarchy. It's kind of like rap wars. Rap can be sexist. Or it can be empowering and liberating. Depends on the topic."

Odette agreed.

I asked her, "What about the argument that no albures support the status quo because all of them are inversions of the status quo? Therefore, regardless of their sexism or lack thereof, they are a critique of the status quo."

"Disagree."

Because inversions usually end up supporting the status quo. Odette's not wild about the status quo when it comes to what it has to say about women's bodies. Men may use albures to invert their lower status with other men who are lighter skinned or more educated or happier or more employed or less henpecked, but they sure aren't using it to invert their place in the hierarchy of the sexes. Odette, she's going to hang out with men who, when they actually *do it* (and stop talking about it), don't do it according to the lessons of the albur. A conquest? Nope. It's not that she doesn't laugh. She does. She's Mexican. She's Malinche, the multicultural linguist. She knows how to speak in tongues. She can fight with the best of them. But in the end she prefers pure pleasure over that kind of laughter. Pleasure, where no one is violated.

Adrienne added something: "There are a lot of rappers, women and men, who are dedicated to providing an inspirational message of justice without stepping on anyone in the process. That to me can be empowering, as long as the music doesn't suck, in which case it's just annoying and didactic."

I ONCE SPOKE at a scholarly conference about what I had learned at this dinner party. After the presentation a young woman in the front row who had grown up in Mexico but was then living in Santa Fe, New Mexico, told me how she longed for the piropos of Mexico. How lonely she felt in the States. The streets, silent when she walked by a man. No whispers in her ears, no rose petals sprinkled before her. "No one thinks I'm pretty here the way they do in Mexico."

Everyone laughed because, let's face it, even feminism works better with a sense of humor, not to mention a little vanity.

Santiago, a well-known, salt-and-pepper-haired historian, who also grew up in Mexico, had something to add: "I left Mexico because I never learned how to alburear." And this made us all laugh, too, because we hadn't thought what it would be like to be a man in Mexico without the skills of a bilingual, tongue-twisting alburero. He kept his visits to home short.

Others told jokes from elsewhere in Latin America where they had spent time—Cuba, Argentina, Dominican Republic, Puerto Rico. Jokes from around the world. Like the Mexican albures I described, they said.

"Was there banter back and forth? Was there a duel? Was there a winner? Was the loser *chingado*?"

"No. Yes. Sort of."

"Overlap?"

"Yes. But not entirely the same. Because the sexual duel that ends *that* way is the key. It's all in the duel, along with the vocabulary and the absence of madre, that makes it Mexican. The duel makes it fun. The duel makes it serious. It may be a friendly duel. But everyone who finds themselves in one fights to win."

Santiago knew this more than any of us.

THE DINNER AND lesson in albures ended with David confessing.

"There are examples of men who take it to extremes," he said, "so that they alburean at every chance. It's like a drug, once you get to know it and control it well, you can't stop from doing it. You find double meaning, rhythm, and rhyme in everything you see and hear."

I knew exactly what he was saying. After years of reading feminist critiques of art history scholarship I never saw another war monument or skyscraper or any manmade anything that was taller than it was wide without seeing it as a pajarito. Or, rather, a *pajaro,* without the *ito.* More in the superlative than diminutive. At some point my seeing things this way wasn't restricted in the least bit to those shapes and sizes. Cars and motorcycles. Objects that projected any which way into space and time. I couldn't shut it off.

And so for David, Luis, and Tony. And Odette, Adrienne, and Poppy. They all got carried away. Especially, though, David. He'd start, and he couldn't stop on his own.

"Esa de blanco, yo me la atranco" (This one in white, I will cram her tonight). Not pointing to anything or anyone. Just having fun rhyming in this provocative way.

"Esa de rojo, me la cojo" (This one in red, I'll fuck her in bed).

"Esa de azul me chupa el chupirul" (This one in blue. She sucks on my lollipop).

("That last one doesn't rhyme in translation," someone said to me years later. To which she blurted out, "This one in blue. She sucks on my sugary choo-choo.")

David couldn't help himself. He kept going and going, twisting and turning and rolling them off his tongue. And no one could stop him, either.

As for the rest of us, we ate the last of our enchiladas while we listened. With raw enthusiasm we licked the mango and chili from our plates with our fingers and our tongues like children. Uncultivated weeds reaching for the sky, taking over the once groomed field with entropic gusto.

LOST IN *LOS*

WHEN Armando and I were reminiscing on the phone about the extravagant wedding we attended, on my desk in front of me was a giant diagram of the relationships he recalled. I had put the padres of the bride up at the top beside those of the groom, and I had noted who they were, the web of relationships that extended out from them and why the press came to cover their children's wedding. Below them, yet extending out in all directions, were the first, second, third, fourth generations of this and that relative.

The drawing lacked the right angles of a kinship chart and looked instead like a winding road map of connected parents, godparents, and offspring, all living in the paved parts of town.

"The *padres* of the bride?" I asked, when I looked up and out the window of my office.

It was the pest in me.

I knew that *padres* in the plural could mean either fathers or parents, fathers *and* mothers.[1] But to this day, when someone says *padres*, I first hear *fathers*, then I hear *and mothers*, if the context suggests that. It may only take a split second, but I always do a double take.

My daughters don't. They assume *fathers*. There's no double take. I know because they always ask, What happened to the mothers?

That's a good question, I think.

Because "grammar" doesn't just mean grammar. It also means *a can of worms*.

Take the two basic rules that concern Spanish nouns referring to animals, such as humans, that make it possible that *padre*, the word for father, can mean father and mother, both in the plural and in the singular.

"The rule for the *plural*," Juliana Parra explained to her students with their books ajar when I attended one of her classes in a Salt Lake City suburb in March 2006, "is to use *los*, the masculine plural, whenever there is more than one being and one of the two or more beings is male." Women and girls, *madres* and *amigas* (mothers and friends), *doctoras* and *abogadas* (doctors and lawyers), *gatas* and *leonas* (cats and lions), and the like, by themselves, are all *las*. However, those same women and girls are found inside *los,* the masculine plural, when there is one or more *el*'s or males accompanying them. So that one male doctor with one or more female doctors defaults to *los medicos*. It's the rule, with few exceptions.

Hearing that triggers my thinking.

First, I picture ninety-nine mothers dashing together into a building, plumes reaching out of their hats, purses, and scarves. They sit down, cross-legged and upright. They are somewhere in Mexico City or elsewhere in Latin America or Spain, maybe the Bronx. The lights dim. Sequins flicker and flutter. A woman at the podium welcomes them: "Bienvenidas amigas" (Welcome friends)!—in the feminine. There is laughter, clapping, and then stomping. The auditorium fills with the sounds of women's voices. The speaker is well known to everyone there.

From that scenario I conjure a man. He walks into the back of the auditorium. He removes his hat and coat and finds an empty seat in the back.

"Perdón," The woman speaker says. "Bienvenidos amigos"

(Welcome friends)—in the masculine. *Las* ninety-nine *amigas* plus *el* one *amigo* resulted in *los* one hundred *amigos*.

"But the padre hadn't even a quorum, and yet he conducted business," I blurted out with Juliana by my side.

"I'm afraid so," she sympathized. Then she handed me a textbook after we walked back to her office and directed me to articles and exercises she had written for her students.

Juliana came to visit us when we first moved to Maine. She is the niece of a friend of mine. Before arriving in the U.S., she'd been a practicing engineer in Colombia, but found it unsatisfying. When I met her at the airport for the first time, everything on her was tight, painted, and lifted up. She was young and beautiful. Her smile, bewitching. Not one person coming off the plane looked remotely like her. As it turned out, I never saw her in that outfit again. She ran off to L.L. Bean within hours and became a native just like that, except when it snowed, and then nostalgia for warmth and maybe pavement brought out the high heels in her. Her plan was to learn enough English to raise her status at work back home. But instead she met a young man, married him three weeks later, moved to Utah, and found a job teaching Spanish to seventh graders. After that she returned to engineering because numbers and precision were what she loved most.

"It's basic mathematics," Juliana told her students, as she recalled her engineering days back in Cali, Colombia, before becoming a teacher of Spanish in a Salt Lake City suburb, "how *los* comes to be." She felt bad about the masculine default, but bit her tongue the years she taught it, and will bite her tongue again should she teach in the future. Otherwise none of her English-speaking students will ever learn the Spanish language. She showed them how the issue added up.

La + *la* = *las*
El + *el* = *los*
El + *la* = *los*

$El + las = los$
$Los + las = los$

And then she breathed.

"So *los* wins," a student said.

"No, no, no. It isn't about winning and losing. It's about addition." And with that Juliana pointed to their textbooks. "*Los amigos* includes *la amiga* or many *(las) amigas*, if need be. Just as *los padres* includes *la madre* or many *(las) madres*, if there happen to be many. It's an inclusive process, not a competitive one."

Then she said, "*El + la = el,* also," and explained the rule for the *singular.* "The rule here is to use the masculine singular, *el,* to refer to both female and male animals that have a masculine and feminine variant (*el padre, la madre,* or *el perro,* the male dog, *la perra,* the female dog, or *el gato,* the male cat, *la gata,* the female cat). In the unsexed generic, *el padre,* for example, is equivalent to saying, 'the parent.'"

"Is the masculine default in Spanish any different from the masculine default in English?" I asked. Take the word *man.* I am of the mind that man in practice has never included both sexes, even though the English dictionary states that it does. True in theory, in other words, but I don't think so in practice.

"Grammatically, it is true, the masculine includes the feminine. *Implicitly,* anyway," Enrique Yepes, a professor of Romance Languages at Bowdoin College, tells his students. As does Juliana. Then, after sending them to his website for succinct explanations of Spanish grammar, Enrique immediately notes the *explicit exclusion* of the masculine default.[2] What follows each year are philosophical and pragmatic discussions and debates about language and power and about just how *las madres* disappear into *los padres.*

"Why does the feminine become masculine?" Juliana's students asked before, during, and at the end of the discussions. They remained confused.

"To spur debate on the matter," Enrique informs his students how the word *indígena* (indigenous) "is a masculine noun, even though it ends with an -*a*." He explains, "You say 'las indígenas' only when referring to a group of women." With his tongue in his cheek, he adds, "One male seems to make all the difference." This gets his students going for the rest of the day.

"Poof. Like magic," I added when talking to him about it. Not in German or English. Not Russian. But, yes, in Spanish and its neighbors, Italian, French, and Portuguese.

And all I could do, when I pondered the rules that apply to los and el, was to think of a vast right-wing conspiracy—smoke-filled saloons, black jack, cigars, cockfights, dog fights, and run-on sentences about masculine authority. The truth is that I've never liked masculine defaults, except, maybe, in the areas of barbecuing and mowing the lawn.

"I haven't either," Juliana and Enrique said.

"Nor I," Amparo, Juliana's mother, said, a pediatric nurse for over twenty years, now retired, if you can call taking care of a grandchild full-time retirement. She remembered when nurse in the masculine, *el enfermero*, came to be used in her previously all-female profession. As soon as a man took up nursing—voilá—his linguistic supremacy meant that the masculine form of nurse dominated over the feminine, in the singular and in the plural. It's the rule. She loved hearing *las enfermera*s most of her career. She forgot it wasn't the default.

I asked Enrique what would happen if things were switched around and the word (*las*) *madres* became the boss, like the word bees, *las abejas*, feminine, plural, female bees, female *and* male bees, the insect generic. So *las abejas* includes *los zánganos*, the drones. And while *abejas* was one of a handful of examples in the animal kingdom we knew, others include *jirafas, cabras, hormigas, águilas, moscas, ranas, gaviotas, ratas,* and *serpientes* (giraffes, goats, ants, eagles, flies, frogs, seagulls, rats, and serpents), for example. The exceptions begged for more exceptions.

"If there are a few exceptions, there are precedents and with precedents, a possible change of guard. Right?" I turned to Enrique again.

"Absolutely." He directs his students to read the literature of authors who play around with the masculine default, invert it, tip it upside down, launder it inside out. "Take a line from Cristina Peri Rossi's poetry," he says. "Y dijo el profeta: 'Por su sexo las conoceréis,' And the prophet said: 'You'll know them by their sex.'" He clarifies for everyone how "it plays with the biblical 'Por sus frutos los conoceréis,' Ye shall know them by their fruits."[3] Her substituting *las* for *los* in his opinion prevents language from denying the feminine a voice, a presence, from being an exception to the generic masculine norm. Then he hands the floor over to his students.

Enrique has a tough job being the only man among my friends who teaches the Spanish language to English-speaking students. I depend on him a lot to explain the rules, from *his* point of view. Enrique, who is the nicest person you'll ever meet in this world, always says to me, "It's not fair. I know." And sets to fixing the situation, explaining to his students the rules, showing them how others turn them around and how they too can be masters of these linguistic twists and turns, while reading the novels and poetry that he assigns.

FOLLOWING MY VISITS to Juliana's classroom and Enrique's office, I asked other Spanish-speaking friends, Beyti, who was from Peru, and Lilian, who was from Chile, the same questions. "Where do the ninety-nine women go? Do they cease to exist or are they there as before? Or, are they there, but not as before?" Neither of them knew. But together they've been wondering for almost one hundred years.

For Beyti, who had taught kindergarten for twenty years before moving to the United States, it had been an existential dilemma. After she retired from teaching, she used her small pension to attend law school. She wanted to represent women in Peru and their fight for equal pay. But during that first year of law school she started to have visions of her life as a passing train. She was torn. While she wanted to finish law school, she did not want to remain married. She was fed up with housework. Leaving was the only way out. But leaving meant sacrificing, at least for the time being, her career goals.

She was in Peru eating dinner with her family, when it came to her: "My life is whizzing by and I'm not on board. If I get on now, I can leave. If I don't get on now, it will pass me by." So one morning, she grabbed her passport and visa, which she was lucky enough to have, and left for Miami. While she abandoned law school, she also left behind the weight of feeling lost. In Miami some of the burden lifted. And that's when I met her because she was a friend of a friend, who was coming to Maine with her husband to see the fall foliage. They brought her along.

Before leaving her home in Peru, Beyti had acquired some evidence for her existence. She was able to point herself out in family photographs. She knew it was she who cooked her family meals in the kitchen of their house. She was told by her husband and children how much they loved her. Was she wrong, then, to question whether her existence was real or imagined? These thoughts pained her. "Does existence require a name of one's own?" she asked while waiting for her flight.

Beyti remembered strolling as *el padre*, a parent, in the masculine, outdoors with her husband and children, in their small village on the southern coast of Peru. She remembered hearing or thinking she heard, "Your mother, where is she?" She remembered, also, the response. "Oh right there. She's one of our *padres*, one of our parents."

"Look inside the word, there you can find *la madre*, occluded or secluded, perhaps, but not excluded," she reassured herself each time.

But most of the time Beyti felt insecure and spent too much

time, she said retrospectively, looking around and wondering whether she was really there, either as before or at all.

"Excuse me, Señor, Señora, Señorita. You said, 'Good day, *padres*.' Did you mean to include me, the *madre*?" she asked.

When Beyti called her husband and children from Miami for the first time after deciding not to return, they were confused.

"Madre mía. What on earth? How? Where? Seriously, *when* are you coming home?" not believing a word of it.

"Don't know. Maybe never."

"No. No. We *need* you," and they pulled out every saying in their repertoire to entice her home. "You're our mother, our guide, our motor, our flower, our chimney, the engine of our home. *Mamá,* you are the kindling for our fire, and if you are not here in the house, our hearth will grow cold."

But Beyti, while she loved poetry and aphorisms and read and listened to them as much as she could, didn't hear a thing. She hadn't felt included for many years, even on days when she cooked and cleaned for everyone, her daughter, two sons, her husband. Confusion, rather than exclusion, was the reason why. After twenty-eight years of feeling that way, she left, saying, "Good-bye, I'll be back soon," and kissed everyone on her way out the door. She had no plans to return.

"You take care of everyone but yourself," she said of motherhood, as she grabbed a box of saltines, her favorite finger food. "My children are grown. They can now take care of themselves." The saltines snapped inside her mouth.

"No one dreamt I'd leave. Not even I. No. Impossible. Beyti is a *gallina,* a mother hen, with her *pollitos,* her little chicks. She's overly concerned with their well-being. Were they happy at school, in their jobs, studying, excelling? All three of my children, or four if you count my husband. No one dreamt it."

But it wasn't easy for her. When she thought of her family in the evenings, 5,000 miles away, her husband in his fifties, an electrician who roasted chickens on the side for the extra cash, and her children, then in their twenties, college graduates and well employed, living at home, she continued to worry about them, the way a mother does. When she had some cash saved up from the jobs she had found in the States, she wired money back for a cleaning woman to pick up after them, for a cook to leave them something warm on the stove at night, for the phone to keep its dial tone.

For Lilian, a friend Beyti met at a café while visiting us, it was less complicated. The masculine plural was entirely a practical matter, rather than existential. She was single and had no children and was fifteen years younger than Beyti. She grew up in Santiago, Chile. Also she'd had the experience of working for a cruel, wealthy Chilean woman in Miami, which awoke her to a need to go back to school and pursue her passion to make and decorate wedding cakes for a living. She was naturally good at it. It paid well, and her clients not only loved her but, unlike her last boss, also never accused her of stealing when they misplaced things.

Lilian's strategy, when it came to the Spanish plural, was to look at people's faces when they spoke to her. Also, she took note of their gestures. From the faces and hands she would figure out whether she was part of the picture, part of the group they had in mind. But when she really couldn't tell, she asked, "Am I, your *amiga*, included with *los amigos* you have invited to the party? Or is it boys night out?"

Existential or practical, all six of us—Lilian, Beyti, Amparo, Juliana, Enrique, and I—not to mention others, over the past nine years, have talked about how women in the Spanish-speaking world go about their daily lives having to guess, "Are we part of the *los* or not?" How girls and women attend functions, walk about their neighborhoods, go to the grocery stores, sit in their living rooms, work at their offices and all the while their feminine is collapsed into someone else's masculine when people around them speak in the plural about mixed company. How they have developed an acute sense of context over the millennia. How their peripheral vision must be wider than the horizon, as sharp as a freshly filed pair of scissors.

Beyti is a voracious reader. If she likes a book, she stays up all night to finish it. One evening after she had read all the books she had brought with her, she wondered what she was going to read next. It was a time when Amazon's Spanish titles were limited and our local public library and bookstores had nothing at all in Spanish for adults and only a small selection for children. So I handed her a book I had on my own shelves, *¿Es sexista la lengua española?* by Alvaro García Meseguer, a Spanish engineer living in Madrid who has had a love for linguistics for many years, and said to her, "This might interest you. And when you're done, tell me what you think about what he thinks about the masculine default."[4]

In answering the title's question, Is the Spanish language sexist? García Meseguer said, No, no, no. It isn't. He didn't deny that there was sexism, but he suggested that it was not the fault of the language that women were disappearing in plural and singular situations. Rather, it was the fault of speakers and listeners. The latter, especially, were the ones who were forgetting the implication inherent in the masculine, that is, that a female might be there. In the dictionary, he argued, the definition of words such as *los padres* includes mothers *and* fathers. If listeners forget this, it is a problem within the conversation, not within the language.

After reading the book, Beyti grabbed the dictionary and looked up *padres*. The author was right. *Madre* was in the definition, but not in the first, second, third, fourth, fifth, sixth, seventh, or eighth one provided. But there she was, sure enough, mentioned in the ninth.

"Ninth," she said aloud, as she held the dictionary in her hands.

"Ninth," she mumbled, as she fixed herself a cup of tea.

She agreed with the engineer. It *is* the interlocutors' responsibility for including *madre* when they hear *padres* and especially when a madre or two is there, present somewhere. They are lazy or sexist or whatever for not bothering to go down the list of definitions.

"But listeners don't like to work that hard," Beyti countered.

A handful of psycholinguists have tried to figure out if the masculine defaults of Spanish grammar or the speakers themselves shape perceptions. They have found, after performing systematic tests on randomly selected native speakers of English and Spanish, that there is a gravitational preference for the masculine default in Spanish and in English. Most of the time speakers don't even notice the magnetic pull the masculine has on them. Take pronouns, he and she, *el* and *ella*. The majority of speakers used *he* as the default, even though no grammatical rule requires them to do so.

Furthermore, when speakers in their studies used the masculine pronoun or other masculine defaults, listeners heard and thought of men, and only rarely thought of women. So, while the textbooks and dictionaries included women in the definitions of the male pronouns, few interlocutors actually included them in their minds while they listened and spoke. To top it off, interlocutors conjured up notions of "strong, active, brave, wise, and clever" when they heard or used the masculine *he* and *el*, and conjured up notions of "weak, passive, and foolish," when they used or heard *she* and *ella*.[5]

Preferring the masculine default in either Spanish or English happens very early on. By the age of four my daughters were already referring to their stuffed animals, their blankies, and the like as *he*.

"Could your blankie be a *she*?" I asked one of them.

"Sure," she said. But the next day, she was back to *he*.

And I was back to thinking of a vast right-wing conspiracy that resulted, after ten thousand years of patriarchy, in a genetic predisposition. Because how else could I explain that *my* daughters preferred the masculine default? Her kids maybe. Or his. But *mine*?

"Are you *sure* your blankie isn't a *she*?" I probed.

"Maybe when you're around, Mom, my blankie is a *she*."

"Well, that's a start," I said.

CONSCIOUS OR NOT, the masculine default, as I started to see it, is a problem. It's not only about how it all adds up, but it's also about how it subtracts out. Divides and divvies up. So that disappearances happen with consequences way beyond what one might think.

My favorite example of this comes with the literary excavations of anthropologist Barbara Tedlock, who found that a lot of women shamans, religious practitioners from around the world who communicate with the spirit world, had disappeared in the writings of early twentieth-century Western male scholars. It occurred in the days they used the masculine default while translating from some pronoun-generic Mongolian and Siberian languages into their own pronoun-gendered Romance languages, even while holding in their hands photographs of female shamans, one after another.

Was it a conscious use of the masculine generic? Probably not. But it was a blinded-by-*los* one, and subsequent scholars did not see las inside the los of their predecessors' observations. And with that, there went what should have been a history of women *and* men or, perhaps even, a history of *more women* than *men*. We were left with a fictive history of shamanism, around which an entire subfield of anthropology was shaped, as a result. Until Tedlock came along and reclaimed the lost *las*'s.[6]

And subtraction was what Daysi Magaña Sanchez found when she reported on the *sufragistas'* reading of the Mexican Constitution.[7] Did its founding padres, in using the masculine plural, include the feminine along with the masculine, or was the masculine, well, masculine? Some responded with yes, yes, yes. The *las*'s, the lassies, are there with the *padres*, *hombres, amigos, doctores*, and *abogados*. Absolutely. The *ellas* with the *ellos*.

Okay. So then, why can't we vote? the suffragists asked.

But the men in charge laughed.

Hey, what's so funny? the women asked, not amused.

But for years deep, guttural voices trembled throughout government rooms with high-backed chairs. The voices dropped even
lower, like curtains. Instead of sharing the vote, they threw the
women in jail.

Subtraction is also what Beyti thought happened after she married because attached to her name was now the possessive *de* (of)
followed by her husband's surname. It was another kind of masculine takeover. Beyti Bustos before marriage, Beyti Bustos de García
after marrying Pablo García. After a minute or two recalling this,
while sitting with me in Maine, miles from her family in Peru, she
said that if she were ever to remarry she would use *con* or *contra*,
with or against, but never *de*. That's how she saw it now, focused
on her one aching thought: she wanted a divorce.

"Wow. Marriage. 'Til death do us part. In sickness and in
health.' Does that include with blows to the head and without
them?" She had a grim view of marriage, even though hers had
been a peaceful one. She thought about her husband, for half a
minute. "He'll be fine." And then other half minutes throughout
the days. It's not easy to let go.

"No. No. No." Juliana had a different attitude toward naming. When she married, she adopted her U.S. husband's French
Canadian name, leaving no trace of hers anywhere, except when
it came in handy. She wanted to assimilate. "What's in a name,
anyway?" Except now she makes her son say *amigas* and *amigos*
under all circumstances and in that order.

The Spanish engineer had a suggestion in his concluding
chapters. Here's what to do to change perceptions: Just put "and
women" whenever you can. And never use the male default if there
is an alternative. Use *hombre* only to mean human and qualify the
human as he or she—*hombre varón*, a human man, and *hombre mujer,*
a human woman, if need be. Use *amigos* to mean friends but *amigos
varones* to mean male friends. And so on. Save the masculine plural,
amigos and *abogados*, for the all-inclusive party—only. As for the

feminine singular and plural, they can remain the same because their gender designation is unambiguous.

When Beyti and I thought about this more, we agreed, especially if the rules went beyond salutations. So that the "boys and girls" of "Good morning, boys and girls" would be carried throughout the text. Better yet: "Good morning, girls and boys." And so did Juliana and Enrique, Amparo, and others. "Yes. That is an easy enough prescription for change." After all the Mexican President Vicente Fox had begun to do that, "Welcome *Mexicanas y Mexicanos*," he addressed his listeners (2000–2006). True enough, he was dreadfully mocked for it in the Press. Maybe that's why he resorted to the masculine default in the body of his speeches.

It's not easy to change old habits, but the U.S. women's movement agreed it was worth the effort. One of its foci was to insist the government and businesses place Ms. alongside Mrs. and Miss on forms, in correspondence, in reference to women's titles. Persistence worked. In 1972 the U.S. Government Printing Office approved using Ms. in official government documents. Private enterprise soon followed suit. Then in March 2009, the European Parliament published a pamphlet, "Gender-Neutral Language," asking staff to refrain from using the titles Miss or Mrs., Senora or Senorita, and so on in all the European languages. Just stick to women's full names and professional titles, it recommended. Forget marital status altogether.

And while the theory of language is that it reflects culture, not vice versa, so that a change in culture should create a change in the language, it can't hurt to help language along, while waiting for the rest of the culture to come around. Because, wow, some cultural customs are really stubborn. They could use a push.[8]

ENRIQUE, WHEN HE would say, "I know it's bad," always laughed, and I found myself laughing, too. He's like Pablo in that regard. Whatever the linguistic crime, there is always something funny about it.

This wonderful Romance language, to paraphrase his enthusiasm, is as fluid as a babbling brook, yet as stubborn as the boulders in its bed. He encourages his students to lift up the boulders. It's hard work, but there is more adventure in it, he assures them. Detecting the hidden women, secret affairs, lickety-split exits. There is no excuse for being lazy, for not going down the list of all possible definitions and possible interpretations. You never know who you might find in that ninth definition when you do. And then once you've done that, you can begin to take the las's and the los's and twist them around, a la Peri Rossi and other poets, essayists, and novelists. Language is malleable. He wants them to know that. "Amigas y amigos, we can perform a number of acts on it, in the classroom, in literature, and in everyday practice," while handing out next week's assignment.

Then, every once in a while he returns to Colombia where he can take things for granted. Eat *arepas*. Relax.

"In a way," he contemplates later in a computer message to me, relaxed and rested, "because gendered languages like Spanish make this sexism in language apparent, they have the advantage of making ingrained, everyday forms of exclusion more detectable."

He has a point.

As for Beyti, she sat at the computer every night, writing to all her friends, before she left Maine for California with the vision of owning her own store or working for a union or running a daycare. She watched television with a set of five-pound weights in her hands, which she raised and lowered through several programs. Fingernails painted and polished. The gray in her hair washed away. She was fifty, yet she looked and had the energy of a thirty-year-old. And although she seemed oblivious to it, she had the beauty of a Hollywood movie star. There were no piropos in Maine, but she did turn a lot of heads when she was there.

Beyti made herself at home, while visiting us in Maine. She set up a small altar on the side table: a lamp; a postcard of the Virgin of Guadalupe, which she found in some *rincón* of my farmhouse, resting in a corner; photographs of her children and husband, her parents; a statuette of her patron saint she'd placed in her bag before leaving.

"No, it's not easy to leave," she whispered out loud and was going to rest her head on that thought, when she continued to think. "But, by the grace of God, I jumped aboard my life and stopped looking at it go by, my life as a blur." She fell asleep on that thought. The candle flickering. Her patron saint's silhouette dancing on the ceiling above her.

WHILE SHE VISITED US, Beyti was in the habit of giving me random lessons in grammatical genders or what linguists call "noun classes," in response to our many conversations about feminism and Spanish and my slow learning style. She was a natural teacher, and I was forever mixing them up. One morning, her hands clenched to a hot cup of coffee, still adjusting to the fact of winter up north, she said, "La muerte es femenina." Muerte was one of those exceptions that always threw me because it ended neither with the masculine *o* nor the feminine *a*, as did the majority of nouns in Spanish.

"Yes. Death is feminine," I repeated, wondering, this time, whether there was any more to it than that. And, also, thinking how poetic Spanish sounds to me when I hear it, especially while surrounded by English, up north in Maine.

In Spanish not just nouns that refer to animate beings, but also those that refer to inanimate things, like life and death, house and home, are divided into masculine and feminine. Other nouns, adjectives, articles, and past participles in the sentence or phrase where they appear must agree on their gender. La muerte es femenina (Death is feminine) is an example. Both the article *la* and the adjective *femenina* must agree with the feminine noun muerte.

There has been plenty of disagreement about whether or just how much language or any one part of it influences the way speakers see the world—of how much power, for example, a masculine or feminine noun ending belonging to an *inanimate object* might have over a Spanish speaker.

None, many say.

Including Karen, a Colombian woman living in Maine whom I came to know. For her, she said, la muerte is neither male nor female. It is simply la muerte, a purely grammatical designation. Besides, if she were to picture death as human, she'd probably picture it as male. Maybe due to a U.S. movie she had seen, while growing up in Bogotá, in which the Grim Reaper appeared. Maybe because she's influenced by the English she is now learning. Maybe because she's still only twenty-three.

But then others say, Quite a bit, like Beyti. Or, Without a doubt, like some cognitive scientists who found similar results among speakers describing the *inanimate* world as had been found of speakers describing the *animate* world. Tests within our labs, they say, have shown that German and Spanish speakers map to objects a sex, male or female, in correspondence with the grammatical gender assigned to the *object's* noun. True even when the object was a bridge or a toaster. So that Germans placed images of bridges with culturally feminine terms (*brücke* f. in German) as often as Spanish speakers placed them with masculine ones (*puente*, m. in Spanish).[9]

And then there are those who have a change of mind. Take García Meseguer, who, before publishing his book *¿Es sexista la lengua española?* in which he blamed speakers *and* listeners for their sexist interpretations of grammatical genders and the like, had argued for a more language-responsible psychology in his earlier book, *Lenguaje y discriminación sexual*.[10]

And I think, All of the above.

Because, on the one hand, conversations I have had over the years within a variety of ethnographic laboratories—kitchens, bars, coffee shops, artists' studios, hotel lobbies, and taxis—suggest that most of my Spanish-speaking friends' and acquaintances' mental perceptions of objects are, indeed, influenced by grammatical genders. Although maybe not Karen's. On the other hand, grammatical genders are surely connected to, and at one point in time came from, cultural notions of gender and biological sex. Just as language has had an impact on speakers, speakers have had an ongoing impact on language.

The most likely explanation for the origin of grammatical genders is that they emerged from observations of the environment, female and male animals, which later were mapped to all objects for linguistic or cultural reasons or both. Once that happened, they reinforced those observations. Well, it is a tad more complicated, in that the original ancestral categories for Indo-European languages appear to have been *active* and *not active*, which gave way to masculine and neuter-feminine. Linguists are still trying to piece together just what occurred, why and when.[11]

What is curious is that around the world, some languages contain as many as ten noun classes, which makes having two, masculine and feminine, look simple. And those noun classes may be as diverse as animate-inanimate, human-nonhuman, male-other, liquid-solid, close-far, and/or some mixture of those. The Native American, Australian Aboriginal, and African Bantu languages are examples of that. Which is why the term *noun class* is preferred by linguists today over the earlier term *grammatical genders,* as gender no longer means *genre.* Although for those same reasons, Romance language teachers prefer the term *grammatical genders,* precisely because gender, as in masculine-feminine, is an instance of a noun class that most concerns them. Then there are those languages like Chinese and English that have no noun classes or maybe a vestige of them from a former, Old Mandarin or Old English life. The captain of the ship waved from *her* bow is one of those few remnants left in English.

SOMETIMES I WOULD ask Beyti, "Why all this separation into masculine and feminine in the first place?" just to provoke her into making a funny observation about men. But most of the time I silently tried to memorize the genders of given nouns so I wouldn't give away my confusion and struggle and, for that matter, my feminism. But sometimes I couldn't help myself.

"Because why would death be feminine?"

"What does gender have to do with it?" Beyti put on her sarcastic voice. "The classification of a Spanish noun that refers to an inanimate *thing* has *nada* to do with the referent, as the referent has no natural sex or gender," wagging her finger and dropping her voice with the authority of a grammarian in a Medieval court.

Then she laughed and said, voice back to normal, "Sí. Sí. La muerte. Femenina." Because she couldn't help but map to the referent the gender of the word, as though inanimate referents had biological sex and cultural genders. We weren't talking about amigos and amigas or padres and madres, but death.

And I remembered the famous Mexican *La Catrina*, who is a female representation of death, a skeleton all dressed up with a hat of fresh-picked flowers orbiting around the brim, her dress lacey and freshly starched, her satin purse and shoes glistening in the sun below her long, thin, bony hands and deep, hollow eyes. An anthropomorphized image of death. Also, I told her I had recently seen a T-shirt of the Grim Reaper in drag on a Mexican American man, which I thought was a perfect example of the issue.[12]

"Yes, yes. Death is feminine." Beyti didn't know who *La Catrina* or the Grim Reaper was. Peruvians don't see death as grim, nor do they dress up skeletons the way the Mexicans do in a kind of tra-la-*la muerte*, sending them off to cavort with the living and dance with the dead. But it didn't matter. She agreed, with another image in mind, perhaps. "Yes, yes. Death is feminine," I could hear Beyti say. "The word, *la muerte* as well as its state of being, the event to which it refers. Whether in Mexico or in Peru or

Spain." With that, she slapped her hands together like the fall of a guillotine, and continued.

"Y el parto es masculino," she said. "Childbirth is masculine." Then she showed me the pictures of her children that she carried in her wallet.

"Sí. Sí," I said. "El parto es masculino."

For a moment, a pause.

"Wait a minute," I interjected. "How is that possible?" confusing the word with the referent as much as she and I had with *la muerte*.

Beyti shook her head.

"How on earth could *el parto* be masculine?" And thought how, having undergone a transformation from a near-death experience, known in common parlance as childbirth, I never looked at anyone—not one person, happy or sad, fat or skinny, young or old, nice or mean—again in quite the same way. I remember looking out the hospital window at the rush hour commuters clogging the sidewalks and streets. And later looking out at people during their summer vacations, hoards of them on the beach, people in the lobby of bus stations and train stations, going up elevators to see the view, waiting in line for ice cream. I remember looking at people in the Mexican graveyards on All Soul's Day and All Saint's Day, looking at people all over town. I remember looking at really big men, tall and manly, images of Diego Rivera, David Alfaro Siqueiros, José Clemente Orozco in photographs, presidents and other statesmen.

I thought of all these people as newborns coming down their mother's birth canal, emerging from their mother's vagina, after their mother's contractions, dilations, screams, pain. Her inhales, pushes, exhales. Then hearing, hours later, "It's a boy" or "It's a girl." Air and sunlight for the first time ever, after a dark, aquatic beginning, lasting nine months. I saw people everywhere I looked in this way. All sharing the same beginning. All coming from a woman, their mother. Feminine beginnings.

And then we couldn't help ourselves. Beyti and I went off on a conversational detour, talking about the sex life of Spanish nouns and started randomly listing what came to mind.

"Eyes and lips, masculine; tongues and ears, feminine; trees, sky, and sun, masculine; rain, clouds, and moon, feminine; house, feminine, but home, masculine; kitchen and living room, feminine; bathroom and dining room, masculine; spoon, feminine; knife, masculine; office and secretary, feminine; work, masculine; and table, feminine."

And from the way Beyti spoke, I pictured, as she did, Spanish words—I mean their referents—not only grammatically gendered but biologically sexed. Also, she confessed, gendered with masculinity and femininity. They were *machos* and *caballeros* and *damas,* machos, gentlemen, and ladies and . . .

Stop right there.

. . . and some referents being even sexy.

"Absolutamente. Table, of course, feminine. She's made to serve. She has utility. She's a she. Chair, feminine also. Lamp, rug, towel, bed. Things that we touch, we rest on, walk on, stomp on, that serve others." She started to see a conspiracy, now that she thought about it, and disregarded *el asiento, el tapete, el piso, el pasto* (the seat, carpet, floor, grass)—all masculine. Although she did mention *el* roof over her head back in Peru with her husband and kids, which she had found incarcerating so she left once everyone could fend for themselves.

I RECALLED BEING in Salt Lake City, hearing Juliana introduce to her bewildered students the masculine and feminine noun classes for nouns signifying *inanimate* referents.

"Why is death feminine and birth masculine?" grammatical genders always presenting a difficult topic for native English speakers, unaccustomed to organizing a whole lexicon in this way. "Or *this* feminine and *that* masculine?" they asked, pointing to this and that in the room. So Juliana explained the rules from a series of textbooks she kept on her desk.[13]

"It's all very objective," she said, while keeping a clear distance between the word and its referent, "with grammatical and phonological consequences, but not psychological ones." And then she explained the rules: "Feminine, all female beings and letters of the alphabet. Masculine, all male beings and countries (*los paises*), districts (*los distritos*), territories, rivers, oceans, seas, towns (although not cities), villages, geographical directions, days of the week, months of the year, ships, infinitives, phrases, numbers, words of Greek origin. Feminine, all words ending in *a* except those ending in *ma* and of Greek origin. Masculine, nouns ending in *-n, -o, -r, -s, -e, -l*, all other endings except *-a, -d, -ción, -sión, -tión, -xión, -sis, -it, -is, -iz, -ez*." Juliana continued: "Feminine, all words ending in *-d, -ad, -ud, -dad, -tad, -tud, -ión, -is, -umbre, -ie, -z*, and words with a stressed *ie* and *ue* in the first syllable, like *suerte* and *muerte*, luck and death."

When Juliana finished, her students asked, "But why is death feminine and birth masculine in the first place?"

"The grammatical gender rules are much easier than that," a historian of Spanish told me. "Better to simply focus on sounds, rather than words and meanings," and cited John Bergen's "simplified approach."[14] Because there were really only two that were semantic, that is, related to meaning, yet eight sound-related or phonetic ones. The two semantic ones were: if a noun referred to a male being and no other, it was masculine; if a noun referred to a female being and no other, it was feminine. As for the phonetic rules, the first seven referred to words that ended in *-a, -d, -z, -ión, -umbre, -ie,* and *-is* and were feminine. The eighth referred to all other endings, and those were masculine. That's it.

Of course, there are exceptions. But the exceptions could be understood easily, she explained, by learning two additional rules governing which words were masculine, which feminine. A stressed *a* in the first syllable, regardless of the word's ending, was often—but not always—feminine: *la calle, la cárcel, la clase, la carne,* and so forth (the road, jail, class, meat). Nouns of Greek origin that ended in *-ma* were masculine, *el clima* (the weather), for example. And then another two rules for ambivalent nouns—could be masculine, could be feminine, it depended on the actual situation. For example, the words for witness, *testigo,* and judge, *juez,* can be used with *el* or *la, el testigo* or *la testigo, el juez, la juez.* Although, of course, ninety-nine female witnesses and judges, along with one male, would be *los testigos* and *los juezes.*[15]

There were other exceptions, which you had just better memorize. *Papá,* for example, your dad, masculine, even though it ends in *-a.* Or *mano,* feminine for "hand," even though it ends in *-o.*

And after finishing, she repeated, "Best to focus on the phonetic and not the semantic, what it sounds like and not what it means. Grammatical genders are arbitrarily assigned. When you emphasize that countries and rivers are masculine, you start going off in the semantic direction and you'll be lost. Again, stick to the phonology and the grammar. Not the referents."

"*Arbitrarily* assigned?"

"Yes," agreed another historian of language, with whom I had lunch not long afterward. "Arbitrarily assigned, that is, in terms of semantics. There is no semantic meaning behind death being feminine." Then she went off on the Latin origin of grammatical genders. Like other historians of Spanish, she noted that when the Latin language, brought to the Iberian Peninsula by Roman soldiers, evolved into Spanish, it maintained the Latin gender assignment, except for Latin words in the neuter, which became masculine most of the time, because Spanish did away with the neuter and the Latin neuter sounded like the Spanish masculine most of the time. A phonetic process of assimilation, not a semantic one.

But my friends like Beyti, who are normal people living their lives outside academia, don't see language that way. Objectively. They have other ideas about gender classifications in Spanish. They think, Perhaps grammatical gender assignments in languages are semantically purposeful. Death is feminine and birth is masculine in Spanish for a reason. It has something to do with how people thought about the referents at one point in time, or various points in time, because gender attributions can change over time, be categorized as feminine and later change to the masculine.

Take Gloria's dad. Gloria, who was born and raised on a farm in the coffee-growing regions of Colombia and who was a friend of Juliana's, loved the whole question of grammatical genders and the ongoing discussion of birth-as-masculine and death-as-feminine. And so did her father.

"Death is feminine because it's part of life, which is in the feminine. As is *la mujer*, the woman who creates it," he told her over the phone from Colombia one morning. And he felt sure about this because while he watched his wife give birth to twelve children, he also watched four of them die. His Catholic sisters, who had a little Buddhism in them, agreed, because they believed in *la reencarnación*, which was feminine, too, he told Gloria.

The anthropologist Stanley Brandes, who studied metaphors of masculinity in a village in southern Spain, said that death was feminine there, too. Not just grammatically, but culturally. He sighed when he heard this and asked for an explanation. The villagers put it in plain words, while eating *tapas* at the bar. They told him that death was female because the term *muerte* was feminine. Snakes were female for the same reason. It was that simple.[16]

"NO. NO," JULIANA disagreed. As a teacher of Spanish she tried to stick to the textbook explanation rather than the subjective ethnographic one of babysitting, kitchens and Sunday, family phone calls.

"*La* is not a she, or an actual person, incarnate," she explained to her students and then later that day told me what she had said to calm them down. "*La* really means 'it,' more or less, but in the

feminine. It's a classification. *La* isn't really a gender in the culturally *masculine-feminine* sense." Using the terms masculine-feminine
sent English speakers, who were learning Spanish, into thinking
about cultural gender, masculinities and femininities, and sex.
Why use these terms anyway when only a few of the referents are
naturally sexed?[17]

"The point is that classes of Spanish nouns are grammatically
organized by *la* and *el*, not semantically classified as masculine and
feminine. The semantic links are entirely random." With that she
moved to the next chapter.

Or *nearly* entirely random, she and others, also, say.

So basically if you find yourself a student of Spanish, do the
following: Think word, not referent. Sound, not meaning, when
learning Spanish syntax. *La muerte* is grammatically preceded by
la, *parto* by *el* for reasons having nothing to do with their referents,
death and birth. Humans may later fill in the gaps and think of
men when the sentence is in the masculine, women when in the
feminine. Even if the subject is a snake or death. But it is not the
language, it is the speakers who do that. There's language and
the users' perceptions. The latter is ex post facto not sui generis.

But Beyti and Gloria disagree. They believe that words like
birth and death are classified a certain way on purpose. Beyti
quoted a poet, Hernández-Catá, from a poem that we had both
read, "El mar, la mar, no es lo mismo."[18]

I translated it into English: "The sea, he, the sea, she; they're
not the same." But wondered, maybe the translation is not "The
sea, *he* then *she*," but "The sea as *el*, the sea as *la*." Two different
forms of *it*. And that's it.

Then I had a second thought about the poet's observation.

"Well put," I said to myself, because *mar* is a rare word.

Very few words in Spanish can be used in either the masculine or feminine gender, although most speakers don't know this
because the feminine version is becoming or has become archaic.
Still used by poets, maybe, but that's about it. Nevertheless, *mar*

can be masculine, *el mar*, or it can be feminine, *la mar*, depending upon how the sea is that day. Depending on how you want your listener or your reader to feel about *it*, the sea. A sea in the masculine is not the same as a sea in the feminine. *Margarita, Está linda la mar (Margarita, How Beautiful the Sea)* is the title that Nicaraguan Sergio Ramírez gave to his famous book, which he took from a poem by the Nicaraguan poet Ruben Darío, both referring to a beloved and poetic sea. Sailors know this about the sea, too. To them the sea is *la mar*, in the feminine, to describe its conditions, whether benevolent or malevolent when their boat is far offshore and the seas are high and mighty, for example.[19] Otherwise, the sea is geographical, the North Sea, the Red Sea, and in the masculine.[20]

There are other ambigendered words, or *were* other ambigendered words, with the same denotative meaning, as recently as the twentienth century. True enough, they are found in books more than conversation, with tradition, rather than rules, regulating their use one way or the other. For example,

> *la análisis* and *el análisis* (analysis)
> *ese arte* and *esa arte* (art)
> *la dote* and *el dote* (dowry)
> *la linde* and *el linde* (boundary)
> *la prez* and *el prez* (glory or honor)

There are more . . .

> *la calor* and *el calor* (heat)
> *la color* and *el color* (color)
> *la cutis* and *el cutis* (skin or complexion)
> *la fin* and *el fin* (end)
> *la origen* and *el origen* (origin)
> *la pro* and *el pro* (benefit)
> *la puente* and *el puente* (bridge)

But, in the end, to simplify things, some students of the language have suggested that instructors of Spanish should teach the last seven of these cross-dressing words as masculine, only. The masculine is winning or has won out.

"Why?"

Because they so rarely appear in the feminine anymore—written or spoken.[21]

And that is what happens throughout history with language. When words or grammatical gender assignments slip away from the spoken language, even though they can be found for a time in written form, they eventually fade away from the written language as well. Generations of speakers always have the final word. They are, in the end, in charge, in spite of the efforts of dictionaries and grammars to resist the tides of human pragmatism.

Beyti and Gloria totally disagreed with these decisions. They were with the poet, rather than the programmatically masculine pragmatist. Teach them both as gendered feminine *and* gendered masculine, they thought, in a last-ditch resuscitation effort, for poetry's sake, if nothing else. And then they began to plot their case for poetic justice.

Then Beyti said, "la *muerte*. That must have been made up by men. *La mujer siempre acaba con todo* (Women, they always put an end to everything). In a man's world."

And at first I went with her on this, "They're dark and mysterious. They're witches who devour the living. They are deeply feared. Their preferred mode of transportation, a broom, a whirl, a neighbor's whisper, the dark of night." I thought of *La Llorona*, another symbol of death in Mexico, a woman who goes around at night in Mexico and other parts of Latin America in her white, gossamer gown stealing little boys and girls who are not home in bed—and drowns them. Children are told this story to keep them close to home, from wandering off, and well behaved.

But then I thought again of La Catrina and her broad-brimmed hat full of flowers. Because while La Catrina symbolizes death, she is not exactly dead. Nor is she scary. No more dead or scary, anyway, than most all others who have died. Well, she might be dead, but she's up and about, like a lot of other skeletons in Mexico, at least, women *and* men, by the way, who are seen in paintings and carvings while dancing, playing the guitar, eating, and talking up a storm. Jolly, even. Like Mexican gravesides during the Day of the Dead with their bright, freshly picked orange marigolds and freshly baked breads and sugar skulls, with your name on them if you wish, and the music and large family gatherings and candles burning throughout the night.

We agreed, Beyti and I, that maybe Gloria's dad had it right. Death and life were two sides of the same concept. They were both the same gender, feminine on purpose, rather than arbitrarily.

Spanish, a language organized by a system of *la* and *el*.

AND WHAT OF *el* childbirth? Not Gloria, not myself, not even Gloria's family, not one of us could figure it out.

As far as Gloria was concerned there was not one man she knew who could possibly endure the pain of the shoulders, arms, hands, belly, legs, and feet much less the head of a child emerging from him in the way children do. That's how she put it, as she drove out of the driveway one afternoon to run some errands, leaving me miles from an answer.

Once again I saw all the thousands of people in the streets, in the stations, at their families' gravesides, on airplanes, at restaurants; buying flower; kings and queens, presidents and vice presidents, grammarians and lexicographers; other children, other adults, bosses and employees, academics who are humbled by their research, those who are inflated by it; anyone and everyone. There they were again in my mind, helpless newborns coming down their mother's birth canal, wondering what the heck was happening to them.

I remembered the birth of my children, not so long but painful.

Especially because there was one right after the other. I've forgotten how many minutes apart.

Then a friend of mine who had studied Indo-European languages with passion, especially Russian, every part of its dictionaries, line of its great literature, came up with what I believe is the best answer so far. "Birth is masculine because it concerns male descent lines."

"The patriline." Yes. Yes. And then, as we sat talking in my house in Maine, we heard voices over the water, low and deep. Generations of them pronouncing: This is my child, in case you were wondering. His birth, her birth is a celebration of the continuation of my family. Our name, our honor, our children's legitimacy, our property, our patriarchal ways. After all, it's not just *el parto* that is masculine, but a family of words related to it as well:

el amor (love)
el sexo (sex)
el matrimonio (marriage)
el preñado (pregnancy)
el embarazo (pregnancy)
el parto (childbirth)
el nacimiento (birth)

Gloria's dad, the Colombian father, agreed. "*El* pregnancy, *el* childbirth? *El* love and *el* sex? Because without men there wouldn't be any." It was that simple. His voice sounded sheepish.

Silence.

Gloria wasn't quite sure what to say. She respected her dad, but this time . . .

"It sounds *machista*, doesn't it? But that's how it has been. For as long as I can remember," he said softening the blow.

My historian friends interjected, reminding me that all those words are in the masculine because they came from the Latin, where they were found in the masculine or neuter. "Spanish did not assign these words genders. They came assigned." And then recited their Latin origins.

amor -oris m. (*el amor,* love)

sexus -us m. (*el sexo,* sex)

matrimonium -i n. (*el matrimonio,* marriage)

praegnatus -us, m. (*el preñado,* pregnancy)[22]

partus -us m. (*el parto,* childbirth)

nascentia -ae f. (*el nacimiento,* birth)—the exception

To summarize their position, All roads lead to Rome.[23] (Except for the origin of *el embarazo,* pregnancy, which seems to be rooted in the Arabic *baraza.*)[24]

Okay fine. The gender assignments existed in Latin before Spanish, for all but *matrimonio* and *nacimiento.* But I had two thoughts on that road map. First, as Spanish evolved, it did away with much of Latin's syntax, including noun declensions. This was no small feat, because noun declensions or noun endings not only permeated Latin, but they also housed its grammar. So another grammar had to be devised, which was ordering words in a sentence and adding prepositions and articles to the vocabulary. Also, while these emergent Spanish speakers tossed out Latin's grammar, they kept its masculine and feminine genders, dropped the neuter and changed some of the gendered designations. So, yes, Latin holds the key. But to only one door. Beyond that, there are other doors, going both backward and forward in time.

"Spanish is Latin with some significant give-and-take," I countered, "on the part of the early, proto-Spanish speakers, who exercised agency. Grammatical genders could have gone the way of noun declensions, but they didn't."

The question remains, How did one noun get to be masculine and another feminine in the first place, in Latin or before Latin?

From my point of view, grammatical genders *must* be in cahoots with cultural ideas and social practices of gender (and other issues perhaps), not separate from them. And *must* have been from the get-go. We know this to be true of the lexicon, which grows as new items, concepts, and activities are introduced into a society. If there is no word for "horse" and horses show up on the scene, well, a word is added to the lexicon. Sometimes words are borrowed from the folks who introduced the horses, others are composed from existing words and knowledge. When an engine is built for the first time, and the designers are looking for a word to describe its power, they use horses as their standard of measurement. The lexicon also reflects dominant preferences and prejudices—lots of words to describe the colors of lipstick and women's clothing, lots of words with which to insult mothers in many languages, not only in Spanish. Why would this relationship not be so with other parts of language, grammar included?[25]

My friend who loves Russian said, "Centuries of men have spent centuries of hours in charge of their family's descent." Then she looked up from her work at the kitchen sink, and with a tired face said, "What woman in the Indo-European family has ever had the time to obsess about that?"

She was right. The assignment of legitimacy and honor to individuals and families in combination with patrilineal inheritance laws has been a very, very big deal in Spain for a very, very long time.[26] As it had been in Rome.

After this, it was a hop, skip, and a jump for us to connect back to the rise of patriarchy, monotheism, Judaism, and, finally, Catholicism and the disappearance of the Virgin Mother's body under layers and layers of clothing. And then leap to the many representations of Christ's body, all over Latin America, dripping everywhere with his blood. Sacrificed for all of us.

And, finally, back to Spanish, which is different not radically, but enough to note from French, Italian, Portuguese, and the other Romance languages.[27] In the history of Spanish a man, alive and later dead (*el muerto,* death in the masculine when referring to a corpse), along whose patriline inheritances passed, was the one whose blood was sacred, the one whose blood was life-giving, family establishing, descent making (*el parto*), according to the all-loving and all-powerful and mighty majesties. A child's legitimacy requires a father, not a mother, to establish, up until recently.[28]

"OKAY, EVERYONE, DINNER is served," my Russian-scholar friend said, while I continued thinking about all this.

But once the kids arrived at the table, my evening was mapped out—as was that of my friend's and Gloria's and Beyti's over the years with their own children, their grandchildren, and for a brief period, my children. Gathering the nuts and berries close to home, rather than hunting the big game beyond the horizon, and then rallying the kids to eat, to their baths, teeth, pajamas, books, kisses. Lights out.

Then picking everything up off the floor and putting it away.

Finally, with any luck, working in the office.

Now where was I? I asked myself last night, the night before, tonight, tomorrow, as I collected my thoughts from the floor and put them back onto the tip of my tongue and fingers. And then I began to type, in the dark, *la oscuridad*, on all accounts.

SOUNDING IT OUT

———

O N my return from a summer in Mexico to a fall in Maine in 2008 I spent many evenings sitting alone on my living room couch with the fireplace warming the cold, New England October air. It was a perfect time to pause, and to peel away the layers of gutters, grammars, and sharp-tongued poetry, right down to a core where only basic sounds remained. Because sometimes simplicity is the best route to take while stumbling around.

I was getting closer to understanding madre, wasn't I?

The truth is that I wasn't sure. Because of a catch. The more I learned, the more I felt like Ariadne. I had threaded together conversations, thoughts, and revelations, which were providing me with a guide out of my confusion. But I remained in a labyrinth with some really big, hairy dilemmas.

I decided to pause, start with the sound *m* and add soon enough an *a*. Making it simple, primary.

"Mmmmmm. Aaaaaaa."

And something happened.

I found the first sounds of the word *madre* comforting when they were separated out from the word, apart from its grammatical gender and disengaged from its cultural meaning, sitting there all by themselves. Sound, pure and simple. Endings seemed to be all tied up with agreement and disagreement, dominance and submission. But not beginnings.

"Mmmmmmmmm." And the syllable, "mmmmmm·aaaaaaaa."

"Say it," when my girls wouldn't go to bed. Or to friends later, and any lucky soul who came through my door, my office, a classroom of students, and especially the stream of Latin American friends who visited us in the fall that year. A few days and weeks later I did this to every other person who came into my life. Indiscriminately. I considered it my way of getting a random sample.

"Say *mamá* or mama. With or without the accent."

And they did, with a furrowed brow.

"Now say it again and again."

"Mama. Mama. Mama. Mama."

"Very, very slowly. Relax your brow, shed your doubt."

"Mmmmm·aaaaa·mmm·aaaaa."

"Yes. Just like that."

"Mmmmm·aaaaa·mmm·aaaaa."

"Let the sound take you in its arms. Now say, mmmmmmm."

In the beginning of the word *madre* is a baby's vocalization, *amamama*. Not the first one a baby will make. It often but not always follows several weeks of *kakaka* or *papapa* or *dadada*. But when it comes, it is never just nonsense baby babble, but meaningful sound production. *Amamama*, an etymological history repeated in the life of every speaking infant over the millennia.

I thought of my girls, who did this all the time when they were toddlers, as did other children everywhere. As far back as the time we lived in Africa, before the diaspora, one hundred thousand years ago, according to linguists Pierre J. Bancel and Alain Matthey de l'Etang. "All phonetic, semantic, evolutionary, and behavioural arguments converge to point *PAPA* and *MAMA* kin terms as the *original source of human spoken words*."[1]

The vocalizations were shortened to *mama* as my girls grew and with my help and the help of others.

"That's right. Mama, that's me," mothers have said, again and again and again. After generations and generations *mama* stayed *mama* while also becoming *mater*, and then *madre*, and added to the dictionaries in Spain.

"Here's how," I said to my friends who had a hard time doing it, and started them off on some exercises.

"Begin with a hum. A long, bilabial, two-lipped mmmmmm. You know how to hum, don't you? Just put your lips together and purr, mmmmmm." I couldn't resist putting it that way. "As if something tasted really good. *Chiles en nogada, mole poblano, pasteles de yuca, sancocho* cooked on the open fire outside, a chocolate *bombón*, your mother's milk after waking up hungry, you're six months old. Mmmmmm good."

Then after getting them started, I'd say, "Now open wide and let out a long, deep ah. Until the last bubble of air has left your lungs."

"Aaaaaaaaaa."

"Feel the oral massage as the vibrations of *a* come up from the back of the throat and into your mouth."

"Aaaaaaaaaa."

"Keep going. Muscles relaxed . . ."

"Aaaaaaaaaa."

"All the way home."

And then they felt it, mama as a perfect polarity of sounds, wide open and then completely closed. It's *m*, a consonant that is easy to pronounce, tongue and lips relaxed. And it's *a*, an optimal vowel, easily pronounced, and with the mouth wide open. Even a baby can do it.

"Ma·ma."

"How do you feel?" I asked them, if they hadn't fallen asleep.

Mamá. First a hum, then a song. Mm·aaaaa·mm·aaaaa. *Mamá*, or a variation the world over. Listen to this, and I produced for them an abbreviated list.

In Bengali, *ma*; Polish, *mama*; Persian, *maman*;
Norwegian, *mamma*; Icelandic, *mamma*;
In languages with and without historical connection.
In Swahili, *mama*; Malay, *emak*;
Vietnamese, *me*; Sinhala, *amma*;
Thai, *mae*; Russian, *mamma;* Welsh, *mam*;
English, mama, mom, mum;
French, *maman*; Italian, *mamma*; Korean-*umma*;
Modern Greek, *mama*; Apache, *shimaa*;
Hopi, *maama*; Kobon (New Guinea), *amy*;
Cree, *-mama*; Romanian, *mama*;
Quechua, *mama*; Mandarin, *mama*;
Basque, *ama*; Spanish, *mamá*.

Sometimes with a switch from *m* to *n* or *ng* as the consonant. It doesn't matter. Nasalized vibrations, just the same.

In Hmong, *niam*; Nahuatl, *naan*;
Turkish, *mama, anne, ana*;
Kikuyu (east Africa), *nana*;
Tagalog, *nanay*;
Chechen, *naana*; Dakota, *ena*;
Urdu, *mang*; Hungarian, *anya*.

Not like other words in a language's history that have evolved, revolved, appeared, and sometimes disappeared, and once they have disappeared, rarely have they reappeared naturally. No. Words for *mamá* have stayed more or less the same over time, through crises, in times of peace. Almost always recognizable, a nasalized consonant, an open vowel. With only some exceptions.

Mama is "extraordinarily resistant to phonetic and semantic change," as Bancel and Matthey de l'Etang note.[2]

Why?

Because mama is rooted in the "cogent anatomical and motor

constraints" of children, so that the word remains unchanged over millennia, they answer.[3] *Mmmmmm* and *aaaaaaa*, two very simple sounds to make inside the tiniest of mouths.

"Yes. But there is more," I say to both of them. I can feel it. "Mmmaaammmaaa." *Ommmmmmm*. *Ommmmm*, the first word, the soul, the universe. "Mmmmm·ama," the mother of words, breath, nourishment, life.

IN 1959, THE Russian linguist Roman Jakobson, repeated, "Why mama . . . ?"[4] after hearing anthropologist George Peter Murdock ask the same question when he presented a list of words for mama from languages around the world and had noted to his listeners how remarkably similar the words were worldwide.[5] Jakobson, pondering the phenomenon, suggested that biology must play a role. What else could explain a universal phenomenon if not nature?

Mama, he stated, starts out not as a vocalization but as a baby's nasalized murmur, *mmmm*, made while nursing. And with that observation Jakobson moved the origin of mama closer to its roots, from infant vocalizations to infant murmurs. *Mmmmmm*. The little mouth filled with warm milk. The only sound possible when the mouth is busy eating.

There are plenty of words to remind us of the relationship. In English, a mammal is a breast feeder, and in Hausa and Xhosa and Latin the word for breast is, respectively, *mama,–ama*, and *mamma*. In Spanish it's more elaborate. *Mamar* is a verb that means to suck, *mamario* means mammary, *amamantar* means to suckle, and *mamarse* means to suck too much, to get drunk.[6]

When I first started to learn Spanish I had to write down words that I heard in conversation because I had always learned best by visualizing what I heard, whatever the topic. But then Tecumseh Fitch, an evolutionary biologist of language and animal communication taught me, while he was writing his dissertation, the value of isolating the sounds of words, and from there I began to develop an ear for language and an appreciation for the biology of sound. Back then Tecumseh and I sat for hours making all sorts of sounds, as we opened a bottle of wine.

He had introduced me to the Jakobson and Murdock articles, as he had assembled an exhaustive collection of studies on primate sounds, including those of humans, as background material to his own research for his dissertation on vocal-tract-length perception and the evolution of language. It was the early nineties when I was teaching linguistic anthropology, and on a few occasions I brought these discussions to class with me as a balance to our otherwise culturally oriented approach.

Tecumseh was not interested in phonemes, but *phonesthemes*. Phonemes are generally defined by linguists to be "the smallest unit of meaningful sound," meaningful to the speakers of any one language or group of speakers within a language. But that definition might be equally applied to phonesthemes. Because their difference is an important one, I've wondered since if a definition of the two might better be this: phoneme, the smallest unit of *conventionalized sound*, and phonestheme, the smallest unit of *iconic sound*.

Phonesthemes have never occupied a glamorous place in linguistic research. They are mentioned, but then are swept aside to make room for the next topic, rarely considered significant to *human* communication. In the literature written by linguistic scholars outside the specialty field of phonestheme research, especially those in anthropology, phonesthemes are referred to as "sound symbolism." A common example given is cockadoodledoo or a syllable, such as *sl*, that carries no denotative meaning but is found to occur in words that share similar traits, such as slime, slippery, slide, slither, sly, and sleaze. But phonesthemes are not symbols, so the term "sound symbolism" is misleading. Furthermore, they *are* significant.

In the linguistic literature there are three kinds of sounds or signs, generally identified as indexical, iconic, and symbolic. Each category receives its definition by just how far or near it is to its referent. An index is directly related, the way an outcry results from a punch to someone's stomach or a small footprint in the mud, with five little toes, results from a shoeless child having good, clean fun. An icon, in turn, is one step away from that, such as the word *cockadoodledoo*, an English speaker's imitation of the sound of a rooster. And a symbol is yet another step away, more like a leap away, with a random relationship to its referent, related only by convention rather than by some inherent property.

Symbols have received the lion's share of linguistic and anthropological attention because the bulk of a language's vocabulary has been assumed to have purely symbolic relationships to its referents. This preference, for the study of symbols along with the assumption that only a handful of words in any given language has iconic aspects to it, has roots in an old tradition and religious imperative to designate language distinct from other forms of animal communication, which depend on indexes and icons, grunts and gestures, to get a point across, like I'm hungry and you're in my way or it's dangerous or you're looking pretty tasty.

Biologists have no such preference for either symbols or *homo sapien sapiens*. "Humans," Tecumseh would say to me, "are like other primates in how they manipulate sound for effect." In addition to studying human languages, he spent time listening to primate calling systems and dissecting animal larynxes, and went all over the world to do these studies. He had a passion for pointing out the ape in all of us. He concluded that one way humans manipulate language is with these unconventionalized phonesthemes.

I became convinced. Phonesthemes are critical to understanding language. Their very primitiveness and physicality are unshackled by culture and its conventions. The route to their referents is a direct one, rather than circuitous. More efficient and pure than symbols, instrumental to the very "efficacy of language," as Tecumseh put it.

Tecumseh didn't stop there. Iconic sounds in languages, he continued, not only create sensation but can reference size, colors, activities, evaluations, potencies, and sex.[7]

Imagine.

Small units, compared to the rest of the language outfit, but stuffed to the brim like molecular biology.

Mmmmmm·aaaaaaa. I thought of madre, while reminiscing about those phonestheme discussions. I thought about poets and orators who have known about phonesthemes for millenia—and apes, the hairy ones, way before that.

TWENTY-FIVE HUNDRED YEARS before Jakobson's article, Socrates told his friend Hermogenes, inside Plato's dialogue *Cratylus*, that "real" words are those that are rooted all but biologically to their referents because they "imitate" the nature of the referent. You can hardly tear the two apart, the name and the object or idea to which it refers. And "real" words are "good" words. All others are less good.

Yes, yes, yes, I thought, when I finally read at leisure the entire *Cratylus*, while humming mmmmm in front of the fire, instead of racing through it as I had in graduate school.

Socrates elaborated, "he who by syllables and letters imitates the nature of things, if he gives all that is appropriate will produce a good image, or in other words a name; but if he subtracts or perhaps adds a little, he will make an image but not a good one; whence I infer that some names are well and others ill made."[8]

Imitation is good. That's the paraphrase of what he said.

Mama, mmmmmm·aaaa, pure sensation, I thought, while I was helped along by Jakobson's nursing baby and a mother's milk. I continued on my own. Mama, a word with substance, a word I felt I could touch when I spoke it; a word filled with iconic sound, like many signs of signed languages; a word so directly related to its referent it was practically an appendage of it. Not like the word *horse*, for example, that trots no obvious relationship to the animal. Might as well be *cheval*.

But with *mamá* or mama, different story because it is rooted in the baby's direct experience with a mother's body.

Yes. Deeply delicious.

Liquid, meaty, gutsy. She's physical.

She's pure vibration.

Mmmmmm. Biologically connected.

Mamá, an ecosystem of sound.

I AGREED WITH Socrates. *Real* and, therefore, *good*.

But Socrates' friend, Hermogenes, wasn't so sure about that. He preferred the conventional approach, which afforded greater distance between the name and the thing to which it referred. Imitation is too close to nature and so very far from civilization, horse or cheval are better names for such an animal, he more or less said, and emphasized how nicely organized and structured language is. Cerebral and civilized, separate from the body and nature. That's why and when it's good, Socrates, Hermogenes argued back.

Then Socrates turned to his friend, Cratylus, after whom the dialogue is named, and asked him some questions:

"Do you admit a name to be the representation of a thing?"

"Yes, I do."

"But do you not allow that some nouns are primitive, and some derived?"

"Yes, I do."

"Then if you admit that primitive or first nouns are representations of things, is there any better way of framing representations than by assimilating them to the objects as much as you can; or do you prefer the notion of Hermogenes and of many others, who say that names are conventional, and have a meaning to those who have agreed about them, and who have previous knowledge of the things intended by them, and that convention is the only principle;

and whether you abide by our present convention, or make a new and opposite one, according to which you call small great and great small—that, they would say, makes no difference, if you are only agreed. Which of these two notions do you prefer?"

"Representation by likeness, Socrates, is infinitely better than representation by any chance sign."[9] And so the Socratic method took hold of Cratylus.

But the field of linguistics, when it was founded two-millennia-plus later, did not agree. Instead it armed itself with Hermogenes' position—lock, stock, and barrel.

And so did I, before my listening to Tecumseh and before my girls were born. Back then, when there was a nature-versus-culture debate, while I was a graduate student, I sided with the culture-explains-it group, culture being above, better, more sophisticated, and malleable than biology. I became a cultural anthropologist, fully socialized into the field. Back then, biology was presented as an alternative explanation, most of the time at odds with a cultural one. Not to mention at odds with a feminist one—*women's lives are not biologically determined with or by motherhood* was part of the argument back then.

Then phonesthemes came onto my horizon. Followed by my girls, who pushed me over the edge. Biology was not an alternative explanation, it was a necessary one in certain categories. How else could I explain my children's troublesome behavior if not with "they were born that way," letting me off the hook, and underscoring a certain kinship alliance they had with biology, which included phonesthemes, among other things.

MAMA, JAKOBSON CONTINUED, has roots in a baby's murmur, then grows into a series of vocalizations, which are then conventionalized into the word *mama*. *Mmmmm* to a vocalizing *amama* and shaped into *mama* by a social circle of relatives, with help from the mother and the father, sisters, brothers, and friends or whoever may be around. And then, in Spanish-speaking countries it is given an accent: *mamá*. Listeners expect it. The structures of the language require it. Ama·ama into ma·ma·ma, a vocalization into a culturally acceptable, repeated phoneme, ma·ma.

Conventionalized, but also socialized, Jakobson continued.

The faces of adults peering down on the vocalizing infant, "Mamá," they say, encouraging the change from vowel-consonant to consonant-vowel and pointing to the referent. *Mamá*, I can see her now. She's a smile, she's eyes-on-you, her voice, in a high register, with rhythm and rhyme. "Gootchy gootchy goo," she says, or "cuchi cuch, chuchi," when speaking Spanish.

Mama is for use inside the house. The Spanish *madre*, English *mother*, German *mutter*, Czech *matinka*, Slovak *maminka*, Polish *matka*, Albanian *matrice* are for use outside the house—more formal, more detached from its origins that way.

But then my houseguest and I thought of *ama*, a similar word in Spanish to *mamá*. Ama is a general kind of mamá, but not The Mamá. According to the Spanish dictionaries, *ama* comes from the Latin *amma*, for wet nurse. And so *ama de casa, de cría, de leche, de llaves, de gobierno, de brazos,* a caretaker of the house, the animals, the children, nursing, the purse strings, the budget. One's right arm.[10]

What about *amar*, to love, *amantes*, lovers, *amoroso* and amorous? Did they start out as a baby's nasalized murmur, too, happy to be nurtured with a mother's warm milk or a caretaker's breast and hand? Sometimes following what-appear-to-be links is illuminating, other times, however, it's illusory. We put the two words together and looked at them, *mamá*, your mother, *amante*, your lover. Was their likeness an illusion?

Not for my Mexican friend Julia, it wasn't, who swore that after she married her husband, who used to see her as his *amante*, she became, in his eyes, his *mamá*. And this had led him to expect from her the following: dinner on the table, a clean house, and child care. It has not been good for Julia because she doesn't see her relationship to him that way. She sees a partnership—or used to.

Well, no matter. It might be that in Julia's case, *mamá* and *amante* are related to the early *mmmmm* murmurs of her husband. Maybe not for others, however.

But with mamá and all the other variations from around the world—*anya, nanay, mae, mom,* and the like—the links that tie them together are clear. To cream, buttery and thick, kisses on the forehead and hands, a warm embrace, a memory in a flame that flickers in a votive candle lit after she's gone with a prayer for her soul in front of a caring saint. For generations and generations a soothing nasalized vibration that comes from the belly, rolls over the heart, and onto the vocal chords, up into the head, where it stays for a little while, bringing peace as it moves out into the world.

Mama, enduring for millennia not only for its articulatory simplicity but for its phonesthemic multiplicity.

SHORTLY AFTER MY *mmmm* exercises, I turned to the word *papá.* I tried to hum the first sound, but I couldn't. *Pppppp* doesn't let the air flow like *mmmmm* does. It holds it in, then aahhh releases it in a puff.

"What do you feel when you say 'paaapaaa'?" I asked my girls, at seven years old.

And this is what I got, "You're crazy, Mom."

"Hey. Did Piaget's children and grandchildren call him that?" I asked.

Start out quietly . . . and slowly . . . with or without the accent. A subtle *p*, a long, quiet *ah*. Or instead, declare it by putting your lips together, keeping a tight hold on the air inside and then open wide, let it go, a burst of air, a river of wind, gushing, flushing, splashing, swishing. Not like the serpentine *mmmmmm*, its purr and wake-me-up-later. The sound *p* is pure staccato.

Papá, or a variation around the world, is a consonantal stop, either *p-*, *t-*, *b-*, or *d-*, that is followed by a wide-open vowel. The same basic pattern as mama but with an entirely different outcome.

In Swahili, *baba*; Kikuyu (east Africa), *baba*;
Xhosa (South Africa), *-tata*; Malay, *bapa*;
Tagalog, *tatay*; Romanian, *tata*;
Welsh, *tad*; Urdu, *bap*; Turkish, *baba*;
Pipil (El Salvador), *tatah*; Basque, *aita*;
Koboo (New Guinea), *bap*; Hungarian, *apa*;
Dakota, *ate*; Nahuatl, *ta'*; Luo (Kenya), *baba*;
Apalai (Amazon), *papa*; English, dad;
Chechen (Caucasus), *daa*; Italian, *babbo*;
Icelandic, *pabbi*; Norwegian, *pappa*;
Cree (Canada), *-papa*; French, *papa*;
Persian, *baba*; Latvian, *baba*; Inuit, *ataata*;
Tamil, *appaa*; Abenaki (N. America), *-dadan*;
Mandarin, *baba*; Quechua, *tayta*; Hmong, *tsiv*;
Hebrew, *abba*; Korean, *appa*; Spanish, *papá*.

"Why . . . papa?" Jakobson asked. Had he applied the same logic to papa as he had to mama, he might have explained the consistency in terms of nature. Instead he became intrigued by difference and, also, the order of events and asked, "Which comes first, mama or papa?" as a word with "real" meaning in a child's linguistic life?

Papa comes first, Jakobson answered.

Since then few have disagreed.

"Yup," my physical therapist said when I asked him. His son definitely said papa before he said mama. It didn't seem fair to him, what with all the hours his wife put in meeting his son's every need.

Jakobson cited a linguist who heard his daughter call out to him, papa, in a "thoroughly designative" way three whole months before she called out mama.[11] That is, her use of *papa* was "distant" and "unemotional," detached from the referent, and he explained that the distance of the father to the child establishes a social relationship and signals the change from emotion to convention. Something like Hermogenes' "conventional."

In its early stages, Jakobson explained, mama doesn't have that distance and so is not language. Ama·ama, mama·mama are verbal interjections, emotional, biological, synonymous with hunger and satisfaction. For *mamá* to be a real word, according to Jakobson, it needed to be detached from all that biology, those breasts, those nasalized murmurs.

Hmmm, I wondered.

Not only are mothers the ones who traditionally teach children how to speak, but how did so many children in the history of the world grow up speaking a language when their fathers were nowhere to be found?[12]

Also, does *mamá* ever become detached from hunger and satisfaction and *mmmmm*? My mouth was watering right now with the very thought of my mother's Yorkshire pudding, the way it would rise in the oven like soft rolling hills after the roast beef's fat had reached the right temperature. My own girls now beg me to bake rhubarb pies and maple creams. Mamá, a mantra that also serves meals, pushes the swing, reads out loud, makes *bombones*.

When my twins were three years old, I heard them in the other room. "Ma·ma·ma," filling the air with no intellectual meaning. Pure, unadulterated vocalizations, while they played and ate, in spite of their age, their fluency in two languages. Just for the pleasure of saying it. And then, an entire year later, I heard them again clear as day, "ma·ma·ma."

One other question. Is *papa* really that removed from emotion? I think, p·haaa·p·haaa may be designative, but not thoroughly, with strings attached from the get-go to the referent's nature. Papa is *filled* with affectivity. There's no escaping notice. Besides how does one know that these early *papás* are not synonymous with hunger and satisfaction? *Papá* the hunter. *Papá* the bread and butter. *Papá* the barbecuer, *taquero*, and short-order cook. *Papá*, the guy with a spoon of cereal, flying it like an airplane into your mouth, if you would just open it. By twelve months, when most children start talking, hard food has been part of the program for half the child's life. Mother's milk may still be part of the diet, but so are tamales and tacos.

By the way, the Spanish dictionary has something to say, as well, about this. *Papá* comes from "the sound expressed by the movement of the mouth when eating."[13] *Papar, papear*, verbs meaning to eat, in colloquial Spanish, the dictionary noted, "colloquial," meaning lowbrow.

When Christiane Corbatt, a sculptor whose Swiss family moved to the alpine Andes of Peru before relocating in the United States, heard me describe this, she blurted out, "If not centrifugal, ejaculatory then." We both spit out our food, laughing.

"*Papá*," I went on, now out of control, "sits right there on the brink of the lips, in the front row, ready to jump out of the starting gate, running. *Papá. Primero, principio, prioridad, privilegio, poder*, primary, principle, priority, privilege, power. *El Papa*, the Pope, with a capital *P* and without the accent. They aren't coincidental, all those *p*'s. Are they?"

And there is more biology to the word *papa* than puffs of air and sounds of food. When my daughters were eight months old, they loved the movement of their tongues and lips, putting them into different positions and letting their exhales flow through the various apertures: ata·ata, ada·ada, their first, clear vocalizations; a·pa·pa·pa, aba·aba·aba, others. They repeated these day in and day out. Along with ama·ama, which arrived later. The tongue flapping on the roof of the mouth, as if the mouth were expecting another spoonful of puréed mango—and then craving to spit it out in puffs and splats. Breathing, puffing, flapping, splatting. Symphonic aerobics for infants and toddlers.

"It must feel good," a friend says, "otherwise why would children say it so much?"

I thought of other repetitive bilabial sounds. *Arrepápalo*, a fritter in Spain; *empapujar*, to bother someone in Peru or make them eat too much in Spain; *papada*, a double chin; *despapar*, a horse holding its head too high; *paparse*, to scoff; *papalote*, a kite in Mexico that flies like a colorful bird; *papalotear*, to daydream or soar like a kite or bird on a good, windy (pronounced whhhh·innnn·dy to feel the icon inside) day; *papagayo*, a parrot; *papito, papaíto*, my dad, my poppy. All so much fun for the body to say.

Which is why I have come to see mama and papa as twins, the mirror-image kind. Exactly the same in their opposition. So that while the sound *paa paa* is centrifugal, with two puffs of air physically pushed out, the sound *mama* is centripetal, the air staying put, resonating from within.

And it's all good news. If you were a word, wouldn't you want to be more than an unemotional, thoroughly designative symbol? With just a little emotion inside you, you can expand your lifetime by millenia.

So I have come to ask a variation of the question Jakobson left unanswered, Why pa·pa·pa in the first place?

And here's my answer: it's easy and fun to pronounce. Because of hunger and satisfaction and the smacking and popping of lips. There is no other sound better suited to be co-opted for the job.

There are a lot of sounds out there. But this is the one chosen, or its variation, around the world. As far as we know, it has been true from the beginning of human time, from the beginning of human vocal chords and social groups. From the beginning of naming those closest to us. True, before we had even left Africa.

Ever since, after hearing a·pa·pa·pa coming from the crib, someone has said, "Did you hear that everyone?"

"She's saying *papá*."

"He's saying *papá*."

"Yes. That's me. The butcher, the baker, the candlestick maker. All those gusts of wind, pah-uff, me. I'm here. I'm home. Your papapapa·papá."

Say it one more time. P·haaaa·P·haaaa. Watch the children on the slide, early in the morning. Here she comes. *Papito*, catch me. Now her sister. Lips smacking, anticipating their promised *dulce de leche* ice cream afterward.

And I returned to Socrates fully believing that *good* words are imitative of their referents and deeply, biologically connected to them. Names are not real names if they don't exhibit the nature of things in their pronunciation, is how Socrates put it. That's how I would put it, twenty-three hundred and some years later.

Papá. An ounce of intellectuality to a pound of affectivity. *Real* because of its attachments.

Papá, an awesome word.

And remarkably different from *mamá*.

BACK TO CHURCH

PRONOUNCING *mmmmm* and *ppppp* led me to wonder: if *mamá* and *papá* started out on an equal footing as good, organic sounds with the only difference between them being a hum and a puff of air, then how on earth did *madre*, which emerged from those nasalized vibrations, meditating murmurs, soothing cradle swings, get into such a gigantic idiomatic and grammatical pickle?

Then it occurred to me on my return trip to Mexico in January 2009 that after *mmmmaaaa* was in place, mothers have had little to do with definitions of madre or mother or mutter or mere, for that matter. While it wouldn't be the first time the non-native (men) has been in charge of naming and defining and, in this case, sensationalizing the native (mothers), it might be the only time in the history of Indo-European languages that so many women, close to half the adult population throughout all Indo-European time, or at least since the Greeks, have been unabashedly overlooked as others spun them into definitions—I mean tangled-up knots. Who on earth are these guys talking about? is what I have asked often when reading articles in the paper or hearing slang on the street or listening to a priest in church. And so do all of my Spanish-speaking, women friends.

I had brought Aurora, our Oaxacan babysitter, along with me to run some errands, and we had gone into a few of the city's churches on our way back to the house. Jennie and Avery came along to continue their comparative research, which until then they'd been carrying out with tacos and tamales and flavors of ice cream, while watching lovers wrap themselves around each other on the shaded benches of the city's parks.[1]

"You would never see that in the United States," they would say, licking their *guanabana-citrico* and *tamarindo-chile* sorbets.

I didn't know what to say. They are eight, or were eight this morning. Seeing these sights may have catapulted them into adolescence.

It was noon on a Saturday, and outside the front doors of an enormous church stood a bride and her family. The church of Santo Domingo de Guzmán is a landmark in all of Mexico for its grandeur, size, gold, for the sheer altitude of its nave, for its fully carved, three-dimensional surfaces running the entire length of the church. It's like a giant jewelry box. There's a long list of couples wanting to marry here from as far as Mexico City, saving their coins while they wait. Women in chiffon dresses and men in dark suits stepped into the church, walked down its long aisle to the front and took a seat.

Perfect timing, I thought.

The four of us sauntered in and found an empty pew halfway down. From our seats we could see the grand altar, the daunting height of the six-story nave, its east wall a treasure trove of statues, paintings, and wooden lacework covered with gold. An image of the Virgin of Guadalupe had been placed temporarily onto the chancel from her central position at the main side altar, a Mexican flag beside her. To the right the federal government, with the support of a local, private foundation, had erected four stories of scaffolding for the restoration of the gold-leaf wall that framed her and that had tarnished and flaked thin after hundreds of years.

The wedding party took up the first quarter of the pews. The emptiness behind them was intermittently filled with the sounds of children yawning, crying, wiggling, the footsteps of tourists walking down the far sides, the prayers of a young man kneeling by a side altar, the snoozing of a worker who had been sweeping the patio since daybreak and had come to nap in a corner pew, broom in hand, while the high sun scooped up what was left of the morning shade.

Of all the events that take place in a Mexican Catholic church, weddings are by far my favorite. People are happy at weddings. The windy sound of organ pipes and trained choir voices carrying Schubert, Bach, Brahms, Mozart, Handel, Mendelssohn fills my spirit. The setting, especially if it is a sixteenth-century Mexican church, stops the world from turning with its tranquility. The attire, not only of the bride, the groom, and their entourage of ushers, bridesmaids, ring bearers, and flower girls, but also of the guests, with their hair, nails, shoes—the men's as well as the women's, and especially of the young unmarried señoritas—is like a fashion show.

I don't know why but the closer one gets to a Mexican Catholic church, the lower the necklines and the higher the heels become, a phenomenon that dazzles my eight-year-olds. I find it baffling, given the Church's bandstand against sex and the disembodied attire of its nuns. Maybe it's a sign of the Church's decline in power, although necklines have fallen and risen and fallen with little regard to the Church over the centuries. Maybe it's a reaction to having strict padres, the more the Church reins in on sexuality, the greater the desire to gallop away on the part of the kids. None of this matters to my girls, however, who say, "Mom, when can we wear shoes like that?" This makes me nervous. "What's wrong with rubber boots and turtlenecks?" I say, and then point out the architecture, the music, the grandmothers in attendance.

As it turned out, our uninvited status was a welcome relief to some of the guests, because noontime, middle-class weddings are astonishingly underattended. Even family members are known to show up only at the reception. Guests who sat close by and pegged my daughters and me as outsiders were curious. And this would lead me to confess, "I love the music and I'm writing a book." And then telephone-number exchanges, invitations and clarifications about the bride and groom and who was related to whom and, finally, where I could find the list of weddings scheduled for next week.

Aurora and I put down our shoulder bags that carried food and notebooks. Without my occasional begging, Aurora attended church only on the occurrence of a cousin's wedding or a favored saint's fiesta in her grandmother's village. Priests no longer held a high place in her worldview as they had when she was a little girl. She was like many other young women of her generation, born in the 1980s and '90s, who had come of age hearing one scandal after another surrounding Mexican clergymen, including Father Marcial Maciel Degollado, the founder of the Legionaries of Christ, who had been—but was no longer—on his way to sainthood a few years before I arrived in Oaxaca. Which is why I had to plead with Aurora, along with my girls, to accompany me from time to time. Come see the flower girls, if not the bride. Then a promise of ice cream for the walk home.

We settled into our seats. An organist was sounding a few chords in practice. String instruments were being tuned. I felt at home, the non-Catholic that I am. I grew up with classical music, living only a stone's throw from the Cleveland Symphony, and with my parents' secular devotion to Italian Renaissance art, filled as it is with biblical scenes. Or maybe I felt at home because of Armando. After all, it was Armando who had set me on this course of dropping into weddings so long ago that going to them was like slipping into an old faithful hammock.

Whatever the reason, before the bride came down the aisle I was joyfully adrift in a sea of thought, *papaloteando*, daydreaming like a kite high in a jeweled sky, and wondering what became of the soothing *mmmmm* once *-dre* and, before that, *-ter* showed up. A

retinue of mental notes accompanied me from articles and books
and papers I had read on the history of Spanish, the Church, the
sixteenth century, Colonialism, Nationhood, the State, and the
lists I had made long before that, looking for clues. If I'd been
unable to find the answer to madre's pickle in the street, at the
bar, in Armando's car, in correspondence with Pablo, at hotel desks
with Alberto, over coffee with Beyti and Juliana, or within Spanish
syntax and phonology, perhaps I could find it in the historical past,
the one that's been written down over the millenia.

I JOURNEYED BACK in time with madre as it gestated inside
the Latin *mater* and inside a language that predated those of Latin,
Greek, and Sanskrit. *Ma* plus *-ter*, an ancient sound attached to *-ter.*
Mmmmm, the prehistoric prelude, yes, but not the finale.

Where did the *-ter* of *mater* come from? Is it rooted in earth-
bound words and endings for land, like the *ter* inside *tierra,* Spanish
for land, or *terrain* or, more generically, *matter*?

No one knew.

Like other words that have come directly from their referent's
biology, this one formalized over the millennia, from *mama* to
mater, and in so doing created a space between the referent and the
word, room enough to wedge open and fill with other morphemes,
small linguistic units of semantic meaning, and lots of other roots
and symbols.

After mater entered the vocabulary of adult speakers, it started
to move around on the tongues, minds, and hands of its hosts. It
headed out of western Asia, eastern Anatolia, the Russian steppes,
west to the Mediterranean, south to the Indian Sea, east to the
Pacific Ocean, north to the Arctic, and northwest to the Danube
and onto the Atlantic. A diaspora, pushed along by waves of migration, settlements, warfare, explorations, conquests, colonizing.[2]
Then, from one or many mother tongues, twelve Indo-European
families of languages were born, including Hellenic and Italic,

that developed into Greek and Latin and from the Latin came the Romance languages, Spanish, French, Portuguese, Italian, Sardinian, Galician, Occitan (Provençal), Catalan, Rhaetian, and Romanian.

Two thousand plus years BCE, before the current era, *mater* became first *meter* in Greek, then, more than one thousand years later, *mater* in Italic, and, by the eighth century CE, *madre* in Spanish, which emerged mostly from the Vulgar or spoken Latin of Roman soldiers, who arrived on the Iberian Peninsula as early as 200 BCE, with a sprinkling from the Classical or literary Latin of the Visigoths, who arrived in the fifth century CE.[3] Later came Arabic, brought by the Moors in the eighth century. Seven hundred years later, the *madre* of the kingdom of Castile and the rest of its language became by regal declaration the official language of a newly united peninsula.

The evolution of *ma* into *mater* into *madre* is in part organic, the story of a sound that sprouted roots and stems in warm, fertile soil, and then with sun, wind, rain, and moons turned into a tall, leafy tree. So from Greek's *meter* came metro, metropolis, the mother city or mother country of a colony of ancient Greece. From Italic's *mater* came the Latin *mater*, which grew into *materis, materia*, material, matter and grafted the Greek metropolis and other words to its limbs. *Mater*, organic matter. From Spanish's *madre* came *madera, matrix, matriz*, wood, womb, mold.[4] And maternity, maternal, matriarch, matron, matriculate, matrimony, mattress, materialize, Madrid, Madeira, Madonna, madrepore, madrigal.[5] And mother waters, mother earth, mother of invention, mother tongue. The Greek and Latin roots are still visible, many of them by now mixed with Arabic. The morphing put a smile on my face—an arrangement of connected things, a situation in which something develops, strong and hard as wood and coral, organic and loving, a place to sleep, a lyric poem, a polyphonic song, a source, a necessity, a mother polity.[6]

But the evolution of madre did not stop there, nor did it occur only in peaceful times. If it had, I would never have seen the graffiti about madres on the decrepit wall in Mexico City twenty-two years ago or met Armando or Pablo or Beyti or any number of friends because they would not exist. There would be no madre pickle, at least not the rococo-*loco* one found here in Mexico. I would not be sitting in this jewelry box of a Church, it would not have been built, Aurora would not be with us, the bride we saw as we entered the church would not look like she does, wrapped up in yards and yards of creamy white lace.

Alas. In the sixteenth century, after Spain had grown into an invincible power, after its king Carlos V picked up where the monarchs, *los católicos* Fernando and Isabel, left off, consolidating Spanish while Catholicizing Spain and sending explorers out to the far reaches of the world, and after Carlos V became, as well, the Holy Roman Emperor, madre and the rest of Castilian Spanish of its sixteenth-century day came across the Atlantic under sail, disembarked on the backs of horses, inside the armor of the conquistadores, on the frocks of friars, in the fingers of hands gripped around swords and crosses and Spanish notions of divinity and superiority. Castilian Spanish became the official language, Catholicism the official religion. And madre settled down among the turmoil and upheaval of New Spain and what became known as Mexico, a Spanish variation on the word *mexica*, the indigenous name for the Aztec people.[7]

On second thought, "settled down" is not the best way to describe what happened to madre at that point.

I DID NOT feel the tapping on my shoulder until Aurora nudged me. A wrinkled-faced woman with her young grandson hobbled up to seated wedding guests, including me, wanting our attention. She had an apron wrapped around her, the neck-to-knee-and-around-to-the-back kind that hardworking women wear in Oaxaca to protect their good clothes underneath—maybe their only clothes. Her long silver braids were tied together behind her with a weary red ribbon that hung below them. She reached out her delicate brown hand in my direction and *pidió limosna*, personally solicited an offering for the love of God, the respectful yet common way of saying in Spanish, She begged for money.

"Aurora?" I whispered. "You know the expression *pedir limosna*?" And I explained to her how in English the woman was begging, there was no other way to put it in common prose, a term that exists in Spanish, *mendigar*, but lacks grace for it brings the activity down to earth when it is best imagined above it. After all, *pedir limosna*, collecting alms, is what the Church does, when during its services it passes a basket back and forth and down the aisle among parishioners to solicit contributions. I reached into my pocket and pulled out some coins for the poor woman, who then moved on to others seated in the pews behind us.

It was one of many translations I had contemplated over the years that had me appreciate just how much the Spanish language is a Christian language, filled to the brim with the sensibility and spirit of the Church. If you speak Spanish to communicate with others, then the Church is by your side. Even if you are Jewish, Muslim, Buddhist, or an atheist. But, of course, that wasn't coincidental. They had grown up together, the Church and Spanish, like twins. Even before Catholicism came to the Iberian Peninsula, Spanish was immersed in various forms of Christianity that sowed semantic seeds. Even when Spanish was in its infancy and more a soldier's Latin than Spanish. Even before that, when it was Greek. Even before Jesus, this brotherhood of language and religion was gestating inside the roots of Spanish's linguistic ancestors, in experiences and beliefs carried within the vocabulary and grammar of speakers who were giving up the nomadic life for a more stationary one, cultivating plants and husbanding animals, storing food, building villages and urban centers, divvying up the labor, eventually handing all politics and worship and the writing of sacred documents, including Scripture, the story of Adam and Eve, literature and dictionaries, over to the literati, who were increasingly in charge.[8]

Once Jesus was conceived it continued to be so, just increasingly so.

Earlier I had pondered Spanish's familial relationship to the Church, triggered by words like *cielo* and *limbo* and *pedir limosna*. But now I thought this: All words that evolved into Spanish, or were adopted into it, did so in the context of Christianity and, eventually, Roman Catholicism, which was well established in Spain by the late eleventh century. I wouldn't want to claim that *all* Spanish words owe their sensibilities to the Catholic Church or to the other forms of Christianity in Iberia that predate it,[9] or that Spanish speakers are weighted down by a vocabulary heavily influenced by the Church. "What's your definition of *madre*?" I've asked everyone I know in Mexico. The list of answers is as long as the number of responses because personal experiences expand any received definition. This is true for each and every word in the lexicon. Having said that, however, I have found that the Church—and Christianity more generally—has had more of an impact on the linguistic experiences of speakers living within its reach than any other institution in the history of the Spanish language, especially on its speakers' gendered experiences of language. With a really big-bang impact on kinship terms, the word *madre*, above all.[10]

"How?" Aurora was always curious to hear my non-native-speaking view of the Spanish-speaking world. Or, anyway, she was too polite to say otherwise.

"To the Church, words are flesh. They breathe. They are alive." That was how I saw it, I told her. The Church doesn't make this claim, except in reference to the incarnation of Jesus as the Word of God. Yet it acts it out, not only inside Scripture and exegeses, creeds and canons, councils and epistles where words become doctrine and skeptics are excommunicated, but inside the cool interior spaces of its sanctuaries, through somatic channels, in auditory, visual, olfactory, gustatory, and tactile ways. Via rituals with paintings, sculpture, prayers, music, song, sermons, incense, candles, flowers, confessions, communions during which people have sat, knelt, stood, walked, consumed, communed, while singing and praying, listening and speaking, tasting and drinking, smelling and touching. The flesh that words become is yours, for Christ lives within you. Their ability to breathe and come alive, depends upon you, and has for two millennia.

Even those who rarely attend church here in Mexico in the twenty-first century have been baptized and will likely baptize their children, attend their own First Communion and that of their children, grandchildren, godchildren, and neighbor's children. Even those who say they no longer believe in the Church attend weddings. When they do they recite every single prayer from memory, know when to stand, sit, and pray, hold their arms low and out from their sides, palms of their hands skyward, when reciting *Padre Nuestro*, bring their palms back together and close to their breast when reciting *Ave María*, cross themselves afterward without even knowing they've done so. Because like the period at the end of a sentence or the wave of a hand, a nod, a smile when saying good-bye, there's an uncomfortable feeling of incompletion if gestures are left undone at the end of a prayer. Parishioners do all these things without any aids. They've been doing them from memory since the friars and conquistadores arrived here in 1519. There are no books in Catholic churches here in Mexico, no bibles, no hymnals to open and read. Words within church services would remain lifeless between covers, without the spirit that an oral culture breathes into them.

I WAS ABOUT to drift back to the sixteenth century again when the organist struck the first chords of Mendelssohn's *Wedding March*, popular since Queen Victoria's day, although not initially among

Catholics, and with them the wedding began. Pure music that brought the entire congregation to its feet, as those descending chords are apt to do. It was our cue not only to stand but also to gaze upon the bride, who had begun her way down the aisle, accompanied by an older man. Her father, an uncle, a godfather, an older brother, I didn't know. She was who everyone had come to see, the crown jewel of the marriage ritual, a living Virgin Mary. Her porcelain face was framed by a misty veil. Her youthful hands held a dozen roses. Her wedding dress expanded out from her waist into halos of white lace and satin, which floated down into soft clouds of puffy, white sunlight behind her.

She glided by us, radiating a smile upon us as she made her way to the altar where her fiancée awaited her. I realized there was no need to transport myself mentally to the sixteenth century. I was there already, by being inside the Church of Santo Domingo and witnessing a Catholic wedding, an outward sign of inward grace, instituted by Christ and described in full in the Council of Trent's twenty-fourth session of 1563, Doctrine on the Sacrament of Matrimony. Ever since churches were first built in Mexico, young couples have wed in them, although not in this one as it was part of a monastery rather than a parish, during its early years. Oh, there'd been interruptions, like the War of Independence, and there'd been modifications, like wedding dresses were not white back then and Mendelssohn had not written his famous *March*. But overlooking those, I was at this moment linked to the beginnings of both Spaniards and Spanish in Mexico.

And what came to my twenty-first century mind was this: *la boda*, the word for wedding in Spanish, derived not from *nuptiae,* the word for wedding in Latin, but from *votum, vota*, "a promise to a god, a solemn pledge, a religious engagement, a votive offering, a vow."[11] *Vota*, converted to Catholicism and carried forward into time on the wings of Spanish.

To my mind came these three words as well: *la Virgen Madre*, followed by flesh, breath, life, her spirituality enriched by her sensuality. The sight of her presence, the sounds of her procession, the smell of her roses, the touch of her grace, having an impact on the linguistic experiences of her parishioner's lives.

Madre stayed on in my mind, as a somatic sensation wrapped up into a worldview, while moving about within the drama of stories.

To say the Catholic Church in Mexico is a patriarchal institution would be unnecessary. But it is worth noting that the iconography of a Mexican Catholic church is disproportionately female. Weddings and brides bring this to life. In Mexico images of the Virgin Madre almost always trump any and all images of men, whether of Jesus, male saints, the Holy Spirit, or any number of angels. There, men appear in more variety, but they are outdone by her beauty, size, elaborateness—her central presence. Even in the Church of Santo Domingo, famous for the three-dimensional Dominican brothers covering a large part of its ceiling, the Virgin has her own side *retablo* or altar, four stories of it covered in gold and adorned with paintings and a crucifix, as well as her own separate chapel, the size of most churches.

One can travel all over Spain and its former viceroyalties and never see as many elaborately bedecked and bejeweled Virgins as one will see here in Mexico—neither in number, nor in glory. Yes, in Peru there are many famously ornate ones. In Colombia, too. Argentina, Chile, Bolivia, Ecuador have their share. The Philippines is a runner-up. But Mexico has all of them beat. Marian devotion, the worship of the Virgin Mary in all her forms through song, prayer, writing, painting, sculpture, and shrines, went wild in Mexico.

NOT LONG AGO, in the middle of all my thoughts about churches, I talked to Armando. I described to him what I was thinking about Spanish and Catholicism. This is what he said: "Mexico is *not* Catholic, it's *guadalupano*." Perhaps it was in response to my saying "Catholic" too many times. He had called me from

Puerto Rico where he was on business and had wanted to know how my writing was going. He'd taken an interest in this chapter because of an unlikely turn of events. He had had a falling out with his mother. Indeed, he went off on a toot about it. He's really had it with all this mother worship.

"What happened?" I asked him, while falling off my chair. Because two decades ago he nearly killed me, pointing out each and every Virgin, while flying us up and down the streets of Mexico City, gesturing with both hands simultaneously and looking out the side windows, and even on occasion the back window, with his hands off the wheel. He believed then that I could not possibly understand Mexico or its contemporary art history without meeting every one of them. *Mexicanidad*, the essence of Mexican-ness, boiled down to good tacos and fresh salsa and the Virgin of Guadalupe. No one has to be Catholic or religious to respect and worship the Virgin of Guadalupe, the Spiritual Mother to all Mexicans. But it helps to be Mexican. It was Mexico, not Spain, not other Latin American countries, not the United States or Canada that she blessed when she appeared. Everyone here knows that. Besides, she's not Mary, as some in the Church claim and go on and on about, but a whole separate Virgin unto herself. She's from Mexico through and through. She's the ancient Aztec Goddess, Tonantzín. That's what a poll would surely indicate if conducted here, he would tell me. Then we'd stop and buy a little something for his mother on the way home.

As it turned out, Armando recently learned of an amorous affair his father had had over forty years ago, when Armando was a young boy. Hearing about the affair didn't bother him. What caused him anguish was his realizing, as his thoughts went back in time, that his father had lived under the wrath of his mother ever since, hardly allowed to move to the right or left without her permission.

The story of the affair didn't surprise me. It is so common a narrative around here that you can't work yourself up about any specific case, even when they involve people you know and love. Also, one way to look at it is this: Armando's father was protecting his mother. She was the good mamá of his children, not one of *those madres* you hear about living somewhere in the neighborhood. No. She was one of the "self-abnegating" and "delicate" ones found in twentieth-century Catholic school teachings of *virgencitas* or Mexican cinema from its Golden Age or the State rhetoric of the nineteenth century, played out in the twentieth.[12]

The problem for Armando was that his dad was now dying. With the impending passage, he was revisiting his father's life. What loomed large for him were not his father's indiscretions, if someone wants to put it that way, but his own memories of his mother's private control over her husband. Self-abnegating in public, maybe, but not in private. She was affected by the rhetoric of the Church and State up to a point. After that point, she let him have it. It wasn't his fault. He was just being a good husband, and a man. Society tolerates that discrepancy. Armando would have preferred genuine threats by his mother to leave his father, even her actually leaving, to the way she kept his dad tied down under her watchful eye.

"Anyway, I'm not the first to say that *guadalupanismo* is a *cult*, obsessed with the Virgin of Guadalupe," Armando went on. "God and Jesus hardly count for anything in Mexico."

There are a lot of explanations for it, the most famous being the allure of the story itself, which, if it is the Church, tells of a miraculous appearance in 1531 of the Virgin Mary as Guadalupe on the hillside of Tepeyac in the outskirts of Mexico City, the former Aztec capital. Or, if it is the People, the story is about the miraculous appearance of Tonantzín in the form of the Virgin of Guadalupe. With the building of a church there in the sixteenth century, although with no mention of Guadalupe at the time, the recounting of her story from the seventeenth century on by Church fathers in sermon after sermon, the reproduction of her image in every corner of New Spain, especially the what-became-Mexico part, Marian devotion, with a distinctly Mexican flavor, caught on here.

Skeptics and historians provide the other explanations for guadalupanismo and for the apparition of other Virgins in Mexico, those of Mary in various guises or not, most of which concern political machinations of the Church, the Crown, the State.[13] Her appearance was timely. There were unruly natives, not to mention uncooperative conquistadores, and the Catholic Crown on the other side of the Atlantic Ocean needed to rein everyone in. A loving, self-sacrificing, compassionate mother and madre of miracles was one way to do it. Also, in the New World Guadalupe had a predecessor, the Virgin of Copacabana in the Andes. The Andean Virgin's story appeared in the sixteenth century and was immediately celebrated throughout Latin America from the beginning of the colonial period. It was so close to Guadalupe's story—she appears as an indigenous woman atop a pre-Hispanic sun temple—that, perhaps, she inspired the where-when-who details of Guadalupe's subsequent appearance in church sermons.

In Mexico, however, no one except scholars and, maybe, Protestants and a few young adults listen to skeptics. Even when the Pope-appointed abbot in charge of the basilica declared in 1996 that he no longer believed the story of the Virgin to be true, no guadalupanas or guadalupanos followed him. It's like hearing "God is dead," when you are a believer. Crazy people say that, was the response of most everyone, along with demands for the immediate resignation of the ignominious abbot from his post.

As it turns out the Catholic Reformation may have had a lot to do with the introduction of Marian devotion to Mexico, as well. For during and after the Counter-Reformation, right when the conquistadores were landing on the shores of the New World and setting up shop, Marian devotion in Europe was flourishing. The Council of Trent, an emblem of the Counter-Reformation, made an interesting contribution to its growth. Written over the course of eighteen years, 1545 to 1563, and overseen by a slew of padres, five popes and two Holy Roman Emperors, including Carlos V, five cardinal legates of the Holy See, three patriarchs, thirty-three archbishops, 235 bishops, seven abbots, seven generals of the monastic orders, and 160 doctors of divinity, the Council set into stone a number of codes and canons, prayers and sacraments in a concerted effort to counter the storm that the Protestant Reformation of Martin Luther and John Calvin was brewing.

One of the Council's many results was the official acceptance of an expanded version of the Ave Maria, the second most recited prayer, after the Lord's Prayer, in Western Christendom. The expanded version, which had been around for at least one hundred years before the Council, consisted of not only the two lines found in Scripture (Luke 1:28,42), "Hail [Mary], full of grace, the Lord [Jesus] is with thee. Blessed art thou amongst women and blessed is the fruit of thy womb," but a third line found outside Scripture, that seems to have first appeared in writing in 1495, "Holy Mary, Mother of God, pray for us sinners, now and in the hour of our death. Amen."[14] The Council's addition of nonscripture to the Ave Maria exemplified, according to historian Jaroslav Pelikan, "the dichotomy between the sole authority of Scripture and the development of doctrine through tradition,"[15] and contributed to an unprecedented flood of mariological writings in the seventeenth century.[16]

It was perfect timing for the evangelization of Mexico by Spanish clerics and visitations by Mary.

As for the word *madre*, it was swept along by the deluge. Or, perhaps, madre constituted the deluge. Named it, gave it human form, life, and spirit.

Swept along . . . or constituted. Either way, ecclesiastical drama on both shores of the Atlantic marked madre's entrance in this foreign land.

I DO NOT know if there had ever been a time when Indo-European speaking mothers before the twentieth century had much of a say on how they were described—inside or outside the home—in dictionaries, courtrooms, and temples of worship. By the time the Virgin Mary carried Jesus in her womb, long before Guadalupe's appearance in Mexico and the development of Marian or Virgin devotion here, they had lost hold altogether of the word that named and defined them. By then the public narratives of creation, not only of the world but of all creatures, including children, had become paternal events, rather than maternal ones, unrelated to the bloodied sheets being washed in the river out back by the *co-madres* and *parteras* (midwives) after the child's delivery.

Miraculous?

Absolutely.

Because paternal creation was, and still is, above nature and way beyond it, according to the padres of the Church (and, eventually, the padres of the State).

Of all the padre-discussed-and-described madres inside the Catholic Church, the Virgin and Eve have had more of an influence on definitions of motherhood than all others combined. In my journey with madre, I stopped overlooking something incredible about the legends of these two mothers. Neither one, as it turns out, is or has ever been a story about maternal creation, as much as it has been a story about fathers.[17]

Take Eve, who was produced from and by a man, Adam, who himself was fashioned by another man, God. But there is more to the qué-padre-ness of the story than that. After God banished both Adam and Eve from the Garden of Eden for bad behavior and sent Adam to live a life of toil, He had Eve suffer in childbirth.

Why?

I've never understood the message. Is it that female creation cannot occur with impunity? Why would a benevolent God want to take credit for pain?

Yet God willed more punishment upon Eve than that. He willed the First Mother to live in obedience to Adam, to be ruled by him. With the emergence of the Catholic Church from Judaism, the story of Adam and Eve was adopted and eventually translated from the Greek, which had been translated much earlier from the Hebrew, into Latin and later every possible language in the world and told over and over and over again by Jews and Christians and Muslims. The story of God's creation of the world.

Qué padre to describe great things—sometimes with a heavy hand.

Also take the Virgin Mary. There had been many virgins before her in pre-Christian Greek and Roman times and even before then. But the story of the Virgin Mary marked the first time in history that a virgin's chastity existed "in paradoxical combination with her maternity."[18] Virgin's before her had not become pregnant while remaining virgins. The Virgin Mary was extraordinary for she bore a child and remained *pure*, with God's helping hand, which is why the Church fathers added the last lines to the Ave Maria, not to celebrate the Virgin Mother so much as to give the highest praise to God the Father for bestowing upon Mary the gift of bearing His son. Mary, the Holy Mother of God, became a model of one's faith in God.[19]

The problem is that the two mothers of the church hierarchy are not friends or even yin and yang to one another. They're in opposition like the ends of two magnets. "Eve is *la pecadora*, the sinner, *por excelencia*. And the Virgin is pure and selfless." That's what Aurora told me she was taught ever since she could sit up on her own. She didn't believe in any of it any more. Neither did her friends.

"Will you marry in the Church?" I asked her.

She wasn't sure. But her friends all have.

"Will you baptize your children, if you have them?"

She wasn't sure about that, either. But her friends have all baptized their children. Their parents made them do it, for the sake of the newborn infants. A simple ritual to wash away the original sin into which they were born.

Perhaps this begins to explain the origins of the symbolic

dilemma of madre in Mexico. The Church believes the bride, once married, is Eve, not the Virgin. "The first parent of the human race, under the influence of the divine Spirit," reads the opening of the doctrine on holy matrimony, "pronounced the bond of matrimony perpetual and indissoluble, when he [Adam] said; This [the bride, Eve] now is bone of my bones, and flesh of my flesh."[20] The bride, virginal in her procession to the altar with her father by her side, Eve in her recession from the altar with her husband, Adam, an hour or two later. The bride, implicated and then sandwiched between two mothers from biblical times, between the two opposing forces of Virtue and Transgression.

THERE'S MORE. THERE always is to big dilemmas. Because as creation was wrested from women as a largely paternal event, things happened. Spirituality rose above biology. The term *padre* grew to include more padres, and celibacy entered the picture.

"I have never been able to get a handle on Sex and the Church," I told Armando, and he thought that was hysterically funny.

Why? Because of the irony? Because of the verb I used? I continued, "If you were reading the Doctrine on the Sacrament of Marriage from the sixteenth century, and you came upon a list of Canons within it, and one of them read this way: 'If any one saith, that the marriage state is to be placed above the state of virginity, or of celibacy, and that it is not better and more blessed to remain in virginity, or in celibacy, than to be united in matrimony; let him be anathema,' wouldn't you be perplexed?" Even if the motivation behind it was opposition to Martin Luther, in this case, Luther's insistence that marriage for priests was good.

Armando said, "It reads, 'saith,' not 'doeth,'" and buckled over.

In all the years I have known Armando, I have stayed clear of asking about his personal life, I mean his very personal life. But after his comment I thought, He's got one. Of course, who doesn't? Or at least, who hasn't? no matter what the Church says. Although, there are plenty of couples who do care or whose parents care. Those couples get married in the Church, as soon as possible.

Today, the position the Church takes is this: Celibacy is best, Chastity is second best. Strictly speaking, celibacy means unmarried and includes continence, which means no sex whatsoever. Loosely speaking, it means, Stay away from women. Chastity, on the other hand, assumes marriage and refers to appropriate sex within it with your wife or husband. Of course, this is not a new position for the Church. It goes back to its very beginnings.

But the Church has a history of wavering on these issues, which is why more than a handful of popes had sons, some of whom became popes. Also, a whole lot of priests have married, others have had mistresses. In New Spain priests regularly had women lovers and, consequently, children, all of whom lived openly with their families in a kind of don't-ask-don't-tell way. When the Church wavered the other way, it was often misogynistic. My favorite example is Pope Urban II, who in the eleventh century ordered the wives of priests to be sold into slavery and their children thrown out into the streets. Urban had inherited Pope Gregory VII's Papal Revolution, which drew clear lines between the sacred and secular realms and, among other concerns, redefined marriage, celibacy, and sexuality.[21] Eventually, of course, those in favor of celibacy won, at least in theory, because while sex brings a man down, marriage brings a man way, way down.

To where?

To earth.

Because padre may have started on the ground with the children he sired, and is even defined in church literature and secular dictionaries as "Adam," as "the first parent" as "the originator," and, more generally, the "father of offspring." But as his membership expanded, siring children became irrelevant—also, illicit. So while he became *padre de familias*, head of a family or many families, he might, in fact, not have had children of his own, might not have been the biological father of any of them. But he remained—remains—the head of a line of descent or the head of a town.

He became, since then, political, and maintains counsels and protects. *Padre conscripto*, a senator of ancient Rome, an elder of a legislative assembly, a profession, a city. He's *padre de su patria*, father of his country, a founding father. He's *padre de la patria*, a man who has served the people, deputy to Cortés, a senator. He's the old man in town, called *padre* out of deference. "Buenos dias, padre. ¡Que le vaya bién!" (Good day, Father. I hope all goes well with you).[22] Once he became political and headed a line of descent, biological or not, I thought this: there went *amor, sexo, matrimonio, embarazo, parto*, and *nacimiento* to el padre's grammatically masculine side.

But padre continued upward to become a religious man. Celibacy gave him levity, I mean gravity with which to levitate. It makes no sense, but it is what happened: emancipation from the body, lightness of spirit, weighted by its responsibilities to God. Sometimes he's secluded for religious reasons, a hermit, *padre de los pobres*, a charitable man, *padre de provincia*, the one who has been in the provinces. He is *padre espiritual*, a religious teacher, a guide who leads souls, a confessor who looks after and directs the spirit and conscience of the penitent. He's *padre apostólico*, each of the fathers of the Church who conversed with the apostles and disciples of Christ. He's the seventy theologians in the period from the second to the seventh century whose writing became official church doctrine.

He's *Santo Padre*, each of the first Doctors of the Greek and Latin Church who wrote about the mysteries and the doctrine of religion. He's the Latin Church Fathers Ambrose, Augustine, Gregory, Jerome. He's one of the chief ecclesiastical authorities who wrote in Greek, Athanasius, Basil, Gregory Nazianzen, and John Chrysostom.

He's a dignitary of the church, a superior of a monastery. A priest in the Roman Catholic and Orthodox Church. *Padre de almas*, a prelate, clergyman, or priest of the Christian Church. He is a priest who hears confession. He's *padre del yermo*, an anchorite. He is father of the faithful, Abraham, Mohammed, one of the sultans, his successors. He's Father of God, a bishop. He's the Most Reverend Father in God, an archbishop and a metropolitan.

He is the Most Holy Father, the Pope, *El Papa, Padre* Santo, *Beatísimo Padre.*

He is each of the rosary beads that are larger than the others. He is God. Padre, with a capital *P. Padre Eterno*, the Eternal Father. *Padre Nuestro*, Our Father, the first person of the Trinity, the entire Trinity. He is Father Almighty, the only God, the Creator, His Holiness, Maker of Heaven and Earth.[23]

"Our Father who art in Heaven, Hallowed be thy Name," and the congregation, the bride and groom, everyone I could see, held their arms and hands toward heaven, while the prayer was carried on a monotone up, up, up to God, who resides not within an opposing duality of women, but inside a united trinity of men, with his Son and Holy Spirit.

Part of me just wants to stop right here and summarize all these padres up into a hegemonic, patriarchal, paternalistic, patronizing pantheon of powerful lexicographers, who stole creation from women. Something simple like that.

While that description wouldn't apply to my dad or Armando's dad, anymore than Eve and the Virgin describe any mother I know here in Mexico, including Armando's, it does begin to describe qué padre's popularity and why and how it means all things great. Not to mention the solar system it rests upon to mean it and the ppppp·puffs of air that fill its sails. An everyday expression as common as tacos tied to a very old sensibility. One that constructs *creation*, the *wow* kind, into something paternal, celibate, and almighty.

Just as I was ready to call it a day, I recalled my friend Claudia, a Chilean-Mexican economist who lives in Mexico City, who had said to me, "Wait a minute. Creation is feminine in Spanish,

not masculine, and speakers—me for one—think of *la creación* as
female and a woman."

"Yes. Absolutely," I said, remembering the moment I saw my
twins for the first time. Two umbilical cords, two heartbeats, forty
fingers and toes. Their little ovaries filled with eggs. There's a reason why people never mention the rooster when they ask, What
came first, the chicken or the egg?

"The problem is, creation was co-opted and then divided in
two, Creation and Pro-creation," I continued, and wondered
aloud, "so, maybe *la* creativity stays in the feminine because of
the muse."

For years on end I used to ask people here, "If this is the land of
mother worship, why not *qué madre* to express greatness, instead of
only *qué padre*?" I still ask, even though I now know the answer.
(I don't count the title of the 2006 TV show, "Qué Madre, Tan
Padre," because the wow of the madre was due to her being *so*
padre.)

"Because men are more *cabrón*," one man put it just the other day,
meaning men are more macho, more motherfucker, son-of-a-bitch,
bastardly. He burst out with laughter. I think because he knew he
was exaggerating wildly and because he knew I knew. "Hey,
cabrón," a man will say to his friend as a term of endearment,
because men can be that way with one another. You get points
for being almighty.

Almighty?

Well, okay, an almighty badass.

MADRE

ONE afternoon in August of 2009, toward the end of our stay in Oaxaca, I pulled over at a lookout point. In front of me, like a kite banner floating across the horizon, were questions I had pondered throughout my journey. Why are idioms with the word *madre* so popular here in Mexico? Where did they come from? What purpose, beyond letting off steam and bonding cuates, do they serve? What keeps them going? Above all, what makes them Mexican?

A stream of related inquiries followed that I had brooded over with the help of Armando, other friends, acquaintances, and complete strangers.

Why in Mexican Spanish is the Virgin's name not used in vain, such as it is in Tuscan Italian (*Puttana Madonna*)? Why are other sacred symbols overlooked, like *Dios* (God) and *hostia* (host), as used in Peninsular Spanish slang, or *tabarnak* (tabernacle) in Quebecois French? And vice versa, Why are there no madre insults in Catholic countries like Italy, home of the Pope, where the Virgin is at least as important as she is in Mexico? Or so few in Colombia, Chile, and Argentina? Why, at the very least, is Eve's name not used in curses in Mexico as it is in other Catholic countries? Eve, a likely candidate, with no need for elaboration.

My attention returned to the blue sky of a typical Oaxacan day. The mountain peaks to the north, east, and south of the city reached up 10,000 feet as they had the day before. The traffic came to a stop at the red light and started up again when it changed to green. And some of the conversations inside those cars included a madre or two, as they did qué padres. I wasn't there, but the odds were. It was, in other words, a totally ordinary day here in Mexico.

Yet it felt extraordinary. Because my journey with madre was flashing before me, the way a life does before one leaves it.

For starters, there were the seeds of Mexico's madres sown, along with the Spanish madres of other countries, in common ground, many thousands of years ago, long before Spanish. Inside the soothing sounds of mmm·aaa that turned into mama and became one of the first two words ever spoken in the ancient prehistory of human language, the other being papa. Inside the -ter and later -dre that are attached thousands of years later to ma-. Inside grammatical genders, el embarazo, el parto, el nacimiento; grammatically consuming plurals, los padres; semantic domains, la vida and la muerte. Inside the ascent and expansion of Castilian Spanish, Spain's Reconquest, the Catholic Church, New World Conquest, and Colonization narratives, especially those accompanied by the Madre of God. Long before all that, they were sown inside the fight-or-flight centers of our primate brains with their capacity to turn words into projectiles, cries into letting-off-steam, names into upside-down-and-inside-out reputations.

Common ground. Yes. Yet there are siblings who have shared the same parents, the same generation, the same dinner table, the same toothbrush, and appear as alike to one another as two strangers after describing each one of those experiences. Because in the variables of a single life lie the resources for difference.

"What happened, then, to the madre of Mexico?" I asked Armando one more time.

But he had just bitten down on a large jalapeño and was trying to find something to drink.

"I think it was the padres," I said. "In a word, if not a nutshell." By that I meant *not only* the nineteenth-century Liberal fathers of Sylvia Arrom's thesis, who cogently demonstrated that it was *they* who were the architects of Mexico's mother cult, *but also* the Church fathers throughout the ages and, yes, Marian devotion. The truth is that I could not for the life of me give up all of Evelyn Stevens' notion that the Virgin was involved, in spite of her misguided reasons for saying so and the evidence Arrom had marshaled against it. Because in my own learning about the anticlerical Liberals and having read their writings, what struck me was how deeply spiritual and religious they were. They remained Catholics, who frequently drew upon Church icons and ideologies, including the Virgin, in their lives and writing, especially when madres were involved.[1]

Benito Juárez, Melchor Ocampo, and Justo Sierra were three liberals I had come to know. Almost daily on my way to the market, I walked by the house where Benito Juárez had lived as a young adult, for it was located, coincidentally, only a few blocks from our rental in Oaxaca and on the very same street. Juárez is the most famous of all the Liberals. As President of the Republic he was responsible for the writing of the Constitution of 1857, which formally wrested power from the Church and set into motion the separation of Church and State. In the house where he stayed, I felt Juárez's story, the one told again and again to schoolchildren: his poor, indigenous beginnings in a rural village in Oaxaca, his rise to become President, his strong belief in nonviolent change. My girls learned more about Juárez in their second grade here in Oaxaca than they learned about anyone or anything else. But what struck me most was what most people don't learn about him: the amorous love letters he sent his wife when she was in exile with their children, having fled yet again from the numerous assassination attempts on her family; the letters he wrote to console her after the deaths of five of their twelve children; and, finally, even how he named his children—José María (Joseph Mary), Guadalupe, Soledad (the name of a famous Virgin in Oaxaca), María de Jesús, among others. It was this information that started me on the path to reading the Liberals' speeches, epistles, and laws, and discovering just how religious and Mary-like, in particular, their descriptions of women were; how, in their scriptures, the Good Mother was substituted for the Virgin, Good Fathers for those of the Church.

"The woman, whose main attributes are self-abnegation, beauty, compassion, shrewdness and tenderness," Ocampo, Juárez's Secretary of the Interior, wrote in reference to the women of Mexico, "must give and shall always give her husband obedience, affability, attention, comfort and advice, treating him with the reverence due to the person who supports and defends us."[2] In 1859 Ocampo's *Epistle* became required reading at the civil ceremonies of state-sanctioned weddings throughout Mexico and remained so until 2007 when the Mexican Senate urged on by feminists, asked the individual states to replace it. (Most have, but Oaxaca has not.)[3] Ocampo's life ended before a firing squad of religious fanatics. But after his death his heart was removed from his body, preserved and put on display like a relic, where it remains to this day in the library of a private school in Morelia, Michoacán, his birthplace.

A subsequent Secretary of Education, Justo Sierra, said this, to a group of women in 1901: "Your calling is to form souls, and to sustain the soul of your husband . . . Dear child, do not become the feminist in our midst . . . While men earn the bread, you are responsible for order, tranquility and the well-being of the home, and above all, you contribute to the formation of souls; this a supreme task . . . shaping souls is better than writing laws."[4] (Later, under another Secretary's watch, the offices of the Secretary of Public Education would be charged with protecting and preserving all church buildings as cultural patrimony.)[5]

When words failed, there was art. *Los Esposos Felices*, the Happy Married Couple, was the title given to a nineteenth-century print published in a popular magazine that pictured an admiring mother with her two adoring children.[6] There was nothing Mexican about the woman. She was Italian, actually, in the image of a Raphael or Michelangelo or Titian *Madonna and Child*. Because even the art that envisioned the Liberal padres' campaign, commissioned or not, identified mothers with the Madonna.

Also, there were laws. Just how hard could a man discipline his wife or how harshly would adulterers be treated in court, especially the husband's wife? The Liberal party, and eventually society, judged that chastity fell on the woman to uphold, as Arrom discovered in court documents, a marked departure from the Church, which saw the sexes equally on this issue.

The heirs of the Liberal agenda, the Revolutionaries of the twentieth century, added rituals and altars in the form of Mother's Day and monuments to the Liberals' rhetoric, pictures, and policies so that the Good Mother of Melchor Ocampo and other Liberal padres turned into a trinity, buttressed on either side by *La Nación* (the State's Virgin Mother, as I saw it) and the Virgin of Guadalupe (the *Nation's* Virgin Mother). Finally, popular culture—and the courts—took care of the rest. Not to mention intellectuals such as Ireneo and Octavio Paz.[7]

No wonder Evelyn Stevens thought the Church and its icons were to blame for this Mother Cult.

ANOTHER QUESTION HAD haunted me, while reading Octavio Paz's essay and taking my list over to Alberto and other friends to see. Was the pathos of the story of Malinche, as told by Paz, another clue to answering, Where do the madres of Mexico come from? What keeps them going? Because around the time Melchor Ocampo was writing his *Epistle*, Malinche was introduced as Mexico's First Bad Mother. Then, after Justo Sierra gave his speech and Mother's Day began to be celebrated twenty years later, Malinche was introduced as Mexico's Eve in the chingada sense.

Yes, the pathos of Malinche's story provides the key, I thought now. Because Catholic narratives, dressed up in secular attire or not, all but require the stigma of a bad mother lurking around them. Esas madres depend on them. For Malinche it was one big flip-flop. Mothers had *not* been exalted before the nineteenth century in Spanish-speaking Mexico, while Malinche had been praised. Malinche, via Paz's interpretations of her, became not only the bad girl of his grandfather's novels, but the *muy, muy* bad girl. While she was important to keeping the narrative of Good Mothers sounding familiar, she was needed, above all, for border control, the way shame stops those who stray, warns those who might.

With Malinche, La Nación, La Virgin de Guadalupe, and the Liberals' Good Mother, Mexico's Madrehood became a constellation united in name, but not in temperament, obedience, or constitution. That's how I summed it up.

So that over the years to come the masculinity of the paternalistic State came to depend upon the virginity of the Nation. Because why else would the State place the Mexican flag beside the Virgin of Guadalupe inside so many churches throughout the country?[8] And why would so many newspaper articles on the influence of foreign ideas and goods into Mexico right up to today be headlined, "Malinchistas, no aceptan productos de casa," (Malinchistas don't like locally made products, they prefer the foreign)?[9] Or *Penetración Cultural* and *Penetración Everything Else* be used to describe the actions of outsiders upon Mexico? Isn't it why Odette's feminism provoked a friend into calling her *malinchista*? Not that she cared. For her, good, healthy disobedience meant opportunity. But the point is that border control by the masculine State of the feminine Nation is a matter of male honor.

That's when I reached for my list, which I had kept handy on my desk. There they all were, most of them homegrown in Mexico, others adopted and adapted from neighbors: me vale madre, un desmadre, va la madre, madre mia, a toda madre, mi madre, tu madre . . .

Shhhhh, came from Propriety in the front room.

. . . worthless, disastrous, awful, wow, a surprise, fuck your fucking mother.

Shhhhh, to no avail.

In jokes, gossip, songs, poetry, prayer, and prose. An ancient sound, a Spanish word, branching off in Mexico in the nineteenth century, going out on a limb in the twentieth.

Alas. Mexico's madre—a little more than kin, and less than kind.

Harboring and arousing within it the idiosyncrasies of its own experience, a somatic sensation, a worldview, sound and flesh, while moving about within the drama of stories into which she has been spun and sung and draped with fabrics so lush and plush I can hardly take my eyes off her.

"*Mamá* may have emerged from the murmurs of babies," I said to my daughters one afternoon while reading them parts of the book, "naturally and unadulterated." *Mmmm*'s pure goodness, *mmmm*'s simple biology. "And if it had stayed that way, I could have written this book in a jiffy."

They would have liked that. More time for play.

"But madre, as a word defined by Church *padres* and adopted more or less wholesale by State *padres* didn't stand a chance," I told them.

For while Juárez, Ocampo, Sierra, and all the other Liberal padres who came to power after Independence were fiercely anticlerical, confiscating the Church's goods and actions by means of the Constitution, they were themselves like Catholic clerics. Because anticlerical in the minds of the Liberals meant: Hand over not only your power and possessions, but your prose and poetry, too; it's now our turn. In the process, the sacred narratives of Fatherhood were secularized, while the secular ones of Motherhood were sanctified. So in the end the padres remained in charge of defining the madres and did so, much as the Church had done, imagining maternity in the hands of the paternal. I don't believe it was all intentional or entirely out of malice. But ¡*Díos Mío*! look what happened. The cult that came to surround motherhood gave birth to a flood of inversions, madres not only for cursing the bad and worshipping the good but madres for all occasions.

"DOES THE POWER of narrative lie in its impact on consciousness?" I asked Armando one evening while trying to finish things
up. I was thinking that it can't be easy to be a mother in Mexico—
balancing stories of chastity, purity, and virginity and taking care of
the kids on a pedestal, all the while inside someone else's definition
of what the whole motherhood enterprise is all about.

"No," he said, "it lies in its impact on children," and then
lapsed into sorrow. His dad had finally succumbed to the cancer,
and because Armando had become estranged from his family, his
mother had not called to tell him of his father's rapid decline in
health. This left him heartbroken, so Armando had gone all over
London in search of a Spanish-speaking priest who could hold a
special mass to memorialize his dad. He found one, he told me, a
Colombian. And thank God. Because this priest helped Armando
bring to a close the chapter of his father's life that was here on earth.

ON OUR LAST day in Mexico, when I heard qué padre for the
umteenth time from a young sales clerk in a small outdoor stand
where we stopped to try on earrings, the artist Laura came back
to mind, twirling around her paintings and casting out qué padres,
more and more exclamation marks, into our conversation.

It was energizing. Qué padre, I went off on my own, for the
way Lola Beltrán sings *Por un Amor*; for how Popocatepetl's snowcapped, volcanic summit peers through the lifting smog during
Easter Week; for the way life used to be in Mexico before all the
kidnappings and drug trafficking; for the way the bakery down
the street sandwiches soft Oaxaca-grown chocolate between two
small clouds of white merengues; for the pyramids of avocadoes
and mangoes in the outdoor markets.

Yes, creativity without the eggs, as we paid for the purchases and
then navigated the sidewalks together, hand-in-hand, skipping on
cobbled stones. And I would have left it at that, alongside so many
unpublished definitions of mother, had Pablo not emailed me. He

was on his way to Providence because as fate will have it, his new job was sending him there on business.

"Where are you?" he wrote.

"Drawing to a close my travels with madre, still here for a few more hours in Oaxaca," I told him, which triggered some back-and-forth reminiscing about the 1990s and those madres that he used to send me over the Internet. Then, true to form, he ended his message to me with a few madres. "I still think that the Mexican political elite *nos ha partido la madre*, have fucked us up, regardless of our so-called democracy. Then, "Todo me vale madre." I pictured the T-shirts sold at Mexican tourist spots of a man, drink in hand, tossing out madres to his right and left about the economy, the country's robber barons, big public scandals—all to make you laugh, not cry.

I burst out laughing, too. Tears ran down my face. Not only because he hadn't changed a bit, but because I saw within his madres, all of them from over the years, the ultimate inversion. Not only were the Paternalistic Fathers turned into Motherfuckers, but the Almighty State into a street-walking, bad, *oh so bad*, worth-nada mother.

Well, there you go. What's good for the goose is good for the gander.

While it's not fair that bad women provide the only representation of bad behavior, practically around the world (bad men almost never do, indeed bad men are applauded much of the time), to see the government in drag right now, while reading Pablo's mail, was to see Pablo having fun, being very, very naughty while winning the albur.

I howled and howled like a little kid, hearing a burp from another child while we sat as best we could at the fancy dinner table, unable to hold in our laughter.

Why do esas madres keep going?

Because those madres that Pablo just sent me, right there on my computer's screen, were such a distillation of the madre constellation, as seen by her children, they were the tequila version.

And because, well, let's face it. Esas madres not only produce daggers, projectiles, and deep sorrow, but in the right place and at the right time they also produce tears of joy and of love, laughter, and forgetting.

"MOM, WE'RE HUNGRY," came from the porch.

Sure enough, our last night in Mexico was upon us. It was time to eat and celebrate. Aurora had passed her entrance exam to nursing school with flying colors. Wearing their new earrings, the girls were swinging on the hammocks outside. As for me, I folded my lists up, back and forth, and tucked them in one of the bags.

From the steamer on the stove, I handed everybody the tamales the girls and I had bought from Mina's grandchildren on our walk home from town. They were the savory results of a well-guarded recipe, passed down from one generation of mothers to another and then to all the children, including the grandsons and grand-daughters who make them now. We opened their cornhusk and banana-leaf wrappers, found inside hand-molded bundles of sweet, ground corn, filled with beans and chicken and hot peppers. And, well, the rest is history inside a very long *mmmmmmmm* that carried itself from the porch, across the neighborhood, over the valley, up the mountains to their peaks, which were disappearing into a purple haze just then from the low rays of the setting sun. When that was done, we let out a long, loud "A TODA MADRE," in unrehearsed unison. Packing with it as much good, healthy dis-obedience and giggles as possible.

And that was how it ended, my journey with madre.

NOTES

WEDDING

1 Michele Morano, *Grammar Lessons: Translating a life in Spain* (Iowa City, IA: University of Iowa Press, 1971), p. 25.

2 *Caelum* was on occasion *caelus*, as some neuter words in Latin, even before Spanish, were moving over to the masculine. Paul M. Lloyd, *From Latin to Spanish* (Philadelphia, PA: American Philosophical Society, 1987), p. 154.

3 Forrest Gander, *A Faithful Existence: Reading, memory and transcendence* (New York: Shoemaker & Hoard, 2005), pp. 70 and 71.

LOVE

1 Arthur Bryson Gerrard, *Cassell's Colloquial Spanish Including Latin American Spanish: A handbook of idiomatic usage*, 3rd rev. ed. (New York: John Wiley & Sons, 1981), p. 99.

2 While mother insults and jokes as well as metaphors of bad mothers are widespread, found in the spoken and written languages of the world, it is assumed they start at the lower end of the class spectrum. I doubt this to be true. In Spanish, for example, Cervantes, in 1613, published his *Coloquio de los perros* (Colloquy of Dogs), in which there is a discussion of mothers as witches and whores. And neurological evidence, also, points to the probability that swearing has no class boundaries. Class comes into play with the teaching of appropriateness and learning when and where to be appropriate.

3 Luisa Puig, *La Realidad Ausente: Teoría y análisis polifónicos de la argu-mentación* (Mexico, D.F.: Universidad Nacional Autónoma de México, 2000), pp. 63–117.

4 Jane Bussey, "The Dark Side of Mexico's Garbage King: Details of sordid sex, corruption are emerging after assassination," *Houston Post*, December 1, 1987, p. 3E. At the time of his death, twenty-seven children were recognized as his. However, by 1995, when Alma Guillermoprieto published her article on him, forty-five children had been recognized as biologically his. Alma Guillermoprieto, *The Heart That Bleeds: Latin America now* (New York: Alfred A. Knopf, 1995).

MIXED MESSAGES

1 In 1950 Octavio Paz credits the use of the term *malinchista* to newspapers. Octavio Paz, *The Labyrinth of Solitude: Life and thought in Mexico* (New York: Grove Press, Inc., 1961 [1950]), p. 86. Discussions with Odette were in the 1990s. In 2009, the term was still widely used by newspapers in Mexico.

2 Alan Riding, *Distant Neighbors* (New York: Alfred A. Knopf, 1985), p. 14.

3 The Mexican madres of this book make their appearance in fiction, as part of the dialogue of characters, in the late 1960s/early 1970s, long after their appearance in the spoken language, some of which may have come from the nineteenth century. Paco Ignacio Taibo II and Carlos Fuentes use "a toda madre" in the late 1980s and early 1990s. See Paco Ignacio Taibo II, *Sombra de la sombra* (Barcelona, Spain: Arte y Literatura, 1989), pp. 56, 219; Carlos Fuentes, *La Frontera de cristal* (Madrid, Spain: Santillana, 1996), pp. 47, 54. Juan García Ordoño uses "dar en la madre" and "importar madres" in the early 1990s. See Juan García Ordoño, *Tres crimines y algo mas* (Mexico City, Mexico: Proxema, 1992), pp. 35, 74. Rafael Bernal uses "una pura madre" in the late 1960s. See Raphael Bernal, *El complot mongol* (Mexico, D.F.: Editorial Joaquín Mortiz, S.A. de C.V., 1969), p. 187. The nonfiction reference to the madres, how-ever, appears earlier. See Octavio Paz, *El Laberinto de la Soledad* (Mexico City, Mexico: Fondo de la Cultura Económica, 1950). References to madres in the language appear in Richard Renaud, *Diccionario de Hispanoamericanismos* (Madrid, Spain: Ediciones Catedra, S.A, 1997).

4 Natalie Angier, "Almost Before We Spoke, We Swore," *The New York Times*, September 20, 2005; Stephen Berger, "Scientists Explore the Basis of Swearing," *Johns Hopkins Newsletter*, October 28, 2005; D. van Lancker and J. L. Cummings, "Expletives: Neurolinguistic and neurobehavioral perspectives on swearing," *Brain Research Reviews* 31 (1999): 83–104.

5 Marta Acevedo, *El 10 de Mayo* (Mexico City, Mexico: SEP, 1982); Eileen Ford, "Children of the Mexican Miracle: Childhood and modernity in Mexico City, 1940–1968," Unpublished dissertation, University of Illinois, Urbana–Champlain, 2008, pp. 89–101.

6 Evelyn P. Stevens, "Marianismo: The other face of machismo in Latin America," in *Female and Male in Latin America*, ed. Ann Pescatelo (Pittsburgh, PA: University of Pittsburgh Press, 1973).

7 Silvia Marina Arrom, *The Women of Mexico City, 1790–1857* (Stanford, CA: Stanford University Press, 1985); Patricia Seed, *To Love, Honor and Obey in Colonial Mexico: Conflicts over marriage choice, 1574–1821* (Stanford, CA: Stanford University Press, 1988).

8 Marcela C. Acevedo, "The Role of Acculturation in Explaining Ethnic Differences in the Prenatal Health Risk Behaviors, Mental Health, and Parenting Beliefs of Mexican American and European American At-Risk Women," *Child Abuse & Neglect* 24, no. 1 (2000): 111–127; Joanna Dreby, "Honor and Virtue: Mexican parenting in the transnational context," *Gender & Society* 20 (February 2006): 32–59; Martha Frías-Armenta and Laura Ann McCloskey, "Determinants of Harsh Parenting in Mexico," *Journal of Abnormal Child Psychology* 26, no. 2 (1998): 129–139.

9 Matthew C. Gutmann, *The Meanings of Macho* (Berkeley, CA: University of California Press, 1996, 2007); Larissa Lomnitz Adler, *A Mexican Elite Family, 1820–1980* (Princeton, NJ: Princeton University Press, 1987).

10 Ireneo Paz, *Amor y suplicio: Novela Historica*, 7th ed. (Mexico City, Mexico: Imprenta y Litografia de Ireneo Paz, 1899 [1873]) and *Doña Marina: Novela Historica* (Mexico City, Mexico: Imprenta y Litografia de Ireneo Paz, 1883).

11 Roger N. Lancaster, "Subject Honor and Object Shame: The

construction of male homosexuality and stigma in Nicaragua," *Ethnology* 27, no. 2 (April 1988): 111–125. See also Jane Collier, *From Duty to Desire: Remaking families in a Spanish village* (Princeton, NJ: Princeton University Press, 1997).

12 For early colonial depictions and descriptions of Malinche, see Liza Bakewell and Byron Ellsworth Hamann, "Painting History in Mesoamerica and Reading Painted History from Mesoamerica: The case of prehispanic Oaxaca and colonial Central Mexico," in *Companion to Mexican History and Culture*, ed. William H. Beezley (Malden, MA: Wiley-Blackwell, forthcoming 2010); Byron Ellsworth Hamann, "Fragmentation and Redemption: The Lienzo de Tlaxcala," paper presented at The Clever Object Research Forum, Session 2, The Courtauld Institute of Art, London, 2009. For an overview of Malinche in history, see Luis Barjau, *La conquista de La Malinche* (Mexico, D.F.: Conaculta, 2009), and an overview of Malinche in literature, see Sandra Messinger Cypess, *La Malinche in Mexican Literature: From History to Myth* (Austin: University of Texas Press, 1991).

13 Angier, "Almost Before We Spoke, We Swore"; Stephen Berger, "Scientists Explore the Basis of Swearing," Jean-Marc Dewaele, "The Emotional Force of Swearwords and Taboo Words in the Speech of Multilinguals," *Journal of Multilingual and Multicultural Development* 25, no. 2 & 3 (2004): 204–222. Also see Steven Pinker, *The Stuff of Thought: Language as a window into human nature* (New York: Viking, The Penguin Group, 2007).

14 Timothy Jay, *Why We Curse: A neuro-psycho-social theory of speech* (Philadelphia: John Benjamins Publishing Co., 2000); also, "The Utility and Ubiquity of Swearwords," *Perspectives on Psychological Science* 4, no. 2 (2009): 153–161; also, *Cursing in America: A psycholinguistic study of dirty language in the courts, in the movies, in the schoolyards and on the streets* (Philadelphia, PA: John Benjamins Publishing Co., 2000). In addition, Richard Dooling, *Blue Streak: Swearing, free speech and sexual harassment* (New York: Random House, 1996); John Fleischman, "When They Put It in Writing, They Were Cursing, not Cussing," *Smithsonian* 27, no. 1 (April 1996): 104–109; Matthew Grimm, "When the Sh★t Hits the Fan," *American Demographics* 25, no. 10 (December 2003): 74 and 75; Elizabeth Arveda Kissling, "'That's Just a Basic Teen-age rule:' Girls' linguistic strategies for managing the menstruation communication

taboo," *Journal of Applied Communication Research* 24 (1996): 209–309;
Maweja Mbaya, "Linguistic Taboo in African Marriage Context," *Nordic Journal of African Studies* 12, no. 2 (2002): 224–235; Ashley Montagu, *The Anatomy of Swearing* (New York: MacMillan, 1967); Paul Rayson, Geoffrey Leech, and Mary Hodges, "Social Differentiation in the Use of English Vocabulary," *International Journal of Corpus Linguistics* 2, no. 1 (1997): 1133–1152; Steven Pinker, "What the F★★★?: Why we curse," *The New Republic* 237, no. 7 (October 8, 2007): 24–29; Karyn Stapleton, "Gender and Swearing: A community practice," *Women and Language* 26, no. 2 (Fall 2003): 22–23.

FOOD FIGHT

1 Zena Moore, "Teaching Culture: A study of piropos," *Hispania* 79, no. 1 (March 1996): 113–120. Also Elizabeth Arveda Kissling, "Street Harassment: The language of sexual terrorism," *Discourse and Society* 2, no. 4 (1991): 451–460; Cynthia Grant Bowman, "Street Harassment and the Informal Ghettoization of Women," *Harvard Law Review* 106, no. 3 (January 1993): 517–580.

2 Odette and others also pointed out that there are many words throughout the Spanish-speaking world, not only Mexico, whose feminine form translates colloquially into "whore." So that *perro*, a male dog, and *perra*, a whore; *toro*, a bull, strong, noble, powerful, and *vaca*, a cow or seal, fat and horrible; *lobo,* a wolf, ferocious, an experienced man, aggressive, and *loba*, a whore; *zorro,* a fox, sly, crafty, intelligent, brave, and *zorra*, a whore; *hombre ambicioso,* an ambitious man, a man with goals, intelligent, and *mujer ambiciosa*, an ambitious woman, a bloodsucker; *un fulano cualquiera*, a man, any man, everyman, and *una cualquiera,* a whore; *caminador,* a man who walks, an active man, and *caminadora*, a streetwalker, a whore; *callejero*, belonging to the street, *callejera*, a streetwalker, a whore; *ligero,* a weak or simple man, and *ligera*, a whore; *hombrezuelo,* a small man, and *mujerzuela,* a small woman, a whore.

3 Hans Wehr, and J. M. Cowan, eds. *The Hans Wehr Dictionary of Modern Written Arabic*, 4th ed. (Wiesbaden, Germany: Otto Harrassowitz, 1994).

4 Albures exist as jokes, as in Mexico, elsewhere, with their own flavor, such as in Puerto Rico. In Nicaragua, however, an albur is an

amorous adventure, an *aventura*. In Puerto Rico and Honduras it is a rumor or a lie. In Cuba an albur is the moment you leave a place precipitously, "de marcharse precipitadamente de un lugar" or it can refer to the final hour of finishing a task, "de la realización de una tarea." Real Academia Española, *Diccionario de la lengua española*, 19th and 20th eds. (Madrid, Spain: Espasa Calpe, 1970, 1984). Notably, in Argentina, while an albur refers to the risk you run in a business deal, it has multiple meanings on the street, which can be found not in dictionaries but in literature. See Federico Wayar, *El Albur* (Buenos Aires, Argentina: Editorial Vinciguerra SRL, 2006).

5 Roger D. Abrahams, *Down Deep in the Jungle: Negro narrative folklore from the streets of Philadelphia* (Hatboro, PA: Folklore Associates, 1964), and "Playing the Dozens," *Journal of American Folklore* 75 (1962): 209–220; Millicent R. Ayoub and Stephen A. Barnett, "Ritualized Verbal Insult in White High School Culture," *The Journal of American Folklore* 78, no. 310 (Oct./Dec., 1965): 337–344; John Dollard, "The Dozens: Dialectic of insult," *American Imago* I (1939): 3–25; Alan Dundes, Jerry Leach, and Bora Özkök, "The Strategy of Turkish Boys' Verbal Dueling Rhymes," *The Journal of American Folklore* 83, no. 329 (July/Sept. 1970): 325–349; Scott Kiesling, "Power and the Language of Men," in *A Cultural Approach to Interpersonal Communication: Essential readings*, ed. Leila Monaghan and Jane Goodman (Malden, MA: Blackwell Publishing Ltd., 2007), pp. 334–350; Thomas Kochman, "The Boundary between Play and Nonplay in Black Verbal Dueling," *Language in Society* 12, no. 3 (September 1983): 329–337; Koeraad Kuiper, "Sporting Formulae in New Zealand English: Two models of male solidarity," in *A Cultural Approach to Interpersonal Communication*; William Labov, "Rules for Ritual Insults," in *Rappin' and Stylin' Out*, ed. T. Kochman (Chicago: University of Illinois Press, 1972), pp. 297–354; Geneva Smitherman, "'If I'm Lyin, I'm Flyin': The game of insult in black language," in *A Cultural Approach to Interpersonal Communication*, pp. 322–330.

6 Adrienne Pine, *Working Hard, Drinking Hard: On violence and survival in Honduras* (Berkeley, CA: University of California Press, 2008).

7 Mary Ellen García, "Influences of Gypsy Caló on Contemporary Spanish Slang," *Hispania* 88, no. 4 (December, 2005): 800–812; Rachel Valentina González, "En los albures yo no com'pito': Identity construction through speech play in Mexican comedic film," unpublished

dissertation, Indiana University, 2007; Victor Hernández, *Antología del albur* (Charleston, SC: BookSurge, 2006); Jennifer Hirsch, "Between the Missionaries' Positions and the Missionary Position: Mexican dirty jokes and the public (sub)version of sexuality," *Critical Matrix: Princeton Working Papers in Feminist Studies* 5 (Spring/Summer 1990): 1–42; Armando Jiménez, *Picardía Mexicana* (Mexico, D.F.: Editorial Andromeda, 1981 [1953]); Cicely Marston, "Gendered Communication among Young People in Mexico: Implications for sexual health interventions," *Social Science & Medicine* 59, no. 3 (August 2004): 445–456; Carlos Monsiváis, *Escenas de Pudor y Liviandad* (Mexico, D.F.: Editorial Grijalbo, 1988); Jack Nakash, *Como dice el refrán: dichos, piropos, malos consejos, albures, etcetera* (Mexico, D.F.: Grijalbo, 2002); Paz, *El Laberinto*; Nicky Santini, *Albures a la Mexicana* (Mexico, D.F.: Selector S.A. de C.V., 2006).

8 The classics: Henri Bergson, *La Risa*, 2nd ed., trans. M. L. Pérez Torres (Madrid, Spain: Editorial Espasa-Calpe, 1986); Mary Douglas, "Jokes," in *Implicit Meanings: Essays in anthropology* (Boston, MA: Routledge & Kegan Paul, 1975), pp. 146–165; Sigmund Freud, *Jokes and their Relation to the Unconscious*, ed. James Strachey (London, New York: Norton and Co., 1960). Some contemporary sources: JoAnne Neff van Aertselaer, "'Aceptarlo con hombría': Representations of masculinity in Spanish political discourse," in *Language and Masculinity,* ed. Sally Johnson and Ulrike Hanna Meinhof (Oxford, UK: Blackwell Publishers Ltd., 1997), pp. 159–172; Joan Pujolar di Cos, "Masculinities in a Multilingual Setting," in *Language and Masculinity,* pp. 86–106.

LOST IN LOS

1 *Parientes*, a related word, refers to relatives, but not to one's parents. See Edith Fahnestock and Mary Bradford Peaks, "A Vulgar Latin Origin for Spanish Padres Meaning 'Father and Mother,'" *Transactions and Proceedings of the American Philological Association* 44 (1913): 77–86.

2 Enrique Yepes, Libro digital *Herramientas de español*: Online Advanced Spanish Book, http://www.bowdoin.edu/~eyepes/newgr/ats/index.html; also see *Oficios del goce: Poesía y debate cultural en Hispanoamérica, 1960–2000* (Medellín, Colombia: Fondo Editorial Universidad EAFIT, 2000).

3 Yepes, *Oficios del goce*, pp. 196–197. Also Cristina Peri Rossi, *Evohé* (New London, CT: Azul Editions, 1994).

4 Alvaro García Meseguer, *¿Es sexista la lengua española?: Una investigación sobre el género grammatical* (Barcelona, Spain: Ediciones Paidós Ibérica, S.A., 1994).

5. D. G. MacKay and T. Konishi, "Personification and the Pronoun Problem," *Women's Studies International Quarterly* 3 (1980): 149–163. Also, Anton Batliner, "The Comprehension of Grammatical and Natural Gender: A cross-linguistic experiment," *Linguistics* 22 (1984): 831–856; Toshi Konishi, "The Semantics of Grammatical Gender: A cross-cultural study," *Journal of Psycholinguistic Research* 22, no. 5 (1993): 519–534, esp. p. 531; D. G. MacKay, "Prescriptive Grammar and the Pronoun Problem," in *Language, Gender and Society*, ed. B. Thorne, C. Kramarae, and N. Henley (London: Newbury House, 1980), pp. 38–53; D. G. MacKay and T. Konishi, "Contraconscious Internal Theories Influence Lexical Choice during Sentence Completion," *Consciousness and Cognition* 3 (1994): 196–222, and "The Selection of Pronouns in Spoken Language Production: An illusion of reference," in *Reflecting Sense: Perception and appearance in literature, culture, and the arts*, ed. F. Burwick and W. Pape (Berlin, Germany: Walter de Gruyter, 1995), pp. 279–300. There are studies that look at the written language as well, such as: George DeMello, "Denotation of Female Sex in Spanish Occupational Nouns: The DRAE revisited," *Hispania* 73, no. 2 (May, 1990): 392–400; Katherine J. Hampares, "Sexism in Spanish Lexicography?" *Hispania* 59, no. 1 (March 1976): 100–109; Giorgio Perissinotto, "Spanish Hombre: Generic or specific?" *Hispania* 66, no. 4 (December 1983): 581–586; S. L. Millard Rosenberg, "Three Little Words We Often See," *The Modern Language Journal* 16, no. 7 (April 1932): 591–609.

6 Barbara Tedlock, *The Woman in the Shaman's Body: Reclaiming the feminine in religion and medicine* (New York: Random House, Inc., 2005).

7 Daysi E. Magaña Sánchez, "El término 'hombre' ¿concepto genérico?" *fem Publicación Feminista Mensual* 13 (September 1989): 81.

8 Maija Blauberg, "An Analysis of Classic Arguments against Changing Sexist Language," *Women's Studies Quarterly* 3 (1980): 135–147.

9 Webb Phillips and Lera Boroditsky, "Can Quirks of Grammar Affect the Way You Think? Grammatical Gender and Object Concepts,"

Proceedings of the Twenty-Fifth Annual Meeting of the Cognitive Science Society, Boston, MA, 2003 (Mahwah, NJ: Lawrence Erlbaum Assoc.), pp. 928–933; Lera Boroditsky, Lauren A. Schmidt, and Webb Phillips, "Sex, Syntax and Semantics," in *Language in Mind: Advances in the study of language and cognition,* ed. Dedre Gentner and Susan Goldin-Meadow (Cambridge, MA: MIT Press, 2003), pp. 1–6. Also, L. Boroditsky, "Does Language Shape Thought? Mandarin and English Speakers' Conceptions of Time," *Cognitive Psychology* 43, no. 1 (2001): 1–22, and "Metaphoric Structuring: Understanding time through spatial metaphors," *Cognition* 75, no. 1 (2000): 1–28; D. G. MacKay, "Gender in English, German, and Other Languages: Problems with the old theory, opportunities for the new," in *Perceiving and Performing Gender: Herstellung und Wahrnehmung von Geschlecht,* ed. U. Pasero and F. Braun (Wiesbaden, Germany: Westdeutscher Verlag, 1999), pp. 73–87; D. Slobin, "From 'Thought and Language' to 'Thinking for Speaking,'" in *Rethinking Linguistic Relativity,* ed. J. Gumperz and S. Levinson (Cambridge, UK: Cambridge University Press, 1996), pp. 70–96.

10 Alvaro García Meseguer, *Lenguaje y discriminación sexual,* 2nd ed. (Barcelona, Spain: Montesinos, 1984). For a discussion that was inspired by Alvaro García Meseguer's work and is dedicated to language and women, see *Mujeres en Red: El periódico feminista,* ed. Monstserrat Boix and Lola Pérez Carracedo (esp. "Lenguaje no sexista"), http://www.nodo50.org/mujeresred/spip.php?article681.

11 H. E. Foundalis, "Evolution of Gender in Indo-European Languages," *Proceedings of the Twenty-Fourth Annual Conference of the Cognitive Science Society,* Fairfax, Virginia, 2002 (Mahwah, NJ: Lawrence Erlbaum Assoc.), pp. 304–322; I. Fodor, "The Origin of Grammatical Gender," *Lingua* 8, no. 1 (1959): 186–214.

12 See also Karl S. Guthke, *The Gender of Death: A cultural history in art and literature* (Cambridge, U.K.: Cambridge University Press, 1999); Claudio Adler Lomnitz, *Death and the Idea of Mexico* (Brooklyn, NY: Zone Books, 2005).

13 William E. Bull, *Spanish for Teachers: Applied linguistics* (New York: The Ronald Press Co., 1965); William E. Bull, Laurel A. Briscoe, and Enrique E. Lamadrid, *Spanish for Communication: Level three* (Boston, MA: Houghton Mifflin Co., 1974); John B. Dalbor, *Beginning College Spanish: From sounds to structures* (New York: Random House, Inc., 1972); Zenia

Sacks Da Silva, *A Concept Approach to Spanish,* 3rd ed. (New York: Harper and Row, 1975); Iris Sinding Dinnes, "Must All Unclassified Spanish Words Be Memorized for Gender?" *Hispania* 54 (September 1971): 487–492; Hayward Keniston, *Spanish Syntax List* (New York: Holt, Rinehart & Winston, 1937); Marathon Montrose Ramsey, *A Textbook of Modern Spanish, As Now Written and Spoken in Castile and the Spanish American Republics,* rev. Robert K. Spaulding (New York: Holt, Rinehart & Winston, 1956); Robert P. Stockwell, J. Donald Bowen, and John W. Martin, *The Grammatical Structures of English and Spanish*, Contrastive Structure Series (Chicago, IL: University of Chicago Press, 1965).

14 John J. Bergen, "A Simplified Approach for Teaching the Gender of Spanish Nouns," *Hispania* 61, no. 4 (December 1978), pp. 865–876.

15 Richard V. Teschner and Yiyuk Estela Alatorre, "The Gender of Spanish Nouns in -s: A description refined," *Hispania* 67, no. 3 (September 1984): 409–411.

16 Stanley Brandes, *Metaphors of Masculinity: Sex and status in Andalusian folklore* (Philadelphia: University of Pennsylvania Press, 1981), p. 81, n. 8.

17 Reference to William Bull's observation in Bergen, "A Simplified Approach for Teaching the Gender of Spanish Nouns," p. 869.

18 Poem by Hernández-Catá (originally published in *La Esfera*) and quoted in Olav K. Lundeberg, "On the Gender of Mar: Precept and practice," *Hispanic Review* 1, no. 4 (October 1933): p. 314. There are many other examples of Spanish-language poems that play with the feminine-masculine forms of *mar*. For example, Antonio Machado in his poem "Profesión de fe"; see Antonio Machado, *Fields of Castile / Campos de Castilla: A dual language book*, ed. Stanley Applebaum (New York: Dover, 2007).

19 Carmencita Delgado de Riso, ed. *Cancionerio: Antologia*, 2nd ed. (Bogota, Colombia: Ediciones Gamma, 1999), p. 68. Also, see Bernice Zamora, "El Ultimo Baile," in *Restless Serpents* (Menlo Park, CA: Diseños Literarios, 1976); Marta Ester Sanchez, *Contemporary Chicana Poetry: A critical approach to an emerging literature* (Berkeley, CA: University of California Press, 1985), p. 256, for a discussion by poet Bernice Zamora about her use of the article "la."

20. The *Diccionario de la Real Academia Española* (*DRAE*) lists many

ambiguous forms of *mar* as well: "1. amb. Masa de agua salada que cubre la mayor parte de la superficie de la Tierra. 2. amb. Cada una de las partes en que se considera dividida. Mar Mediterráneo, Cantábrico. 3. amb. Lago de cierta extensión. Mar Caspio, Muerto. 4. amb. Agitación misma del mar o conjunto de sus olas, y aun el tamaño de estas. 5. amb. Abundancia extraordinaria de ciertas cosas. Lloró un mar de lágrimas." It also lists many feminine forms, including *mar ancha* meaning "high seas," *mar arbolada,* meaning "a strong and agitated sea, with waves greater than six meters high," *mar cerrada* meaning "a sea that is connected to the ocean by canal or some other narrow passageway." *Diccionario de la Real Academia Española (DRAE),* 22nd ed. (Madrid, Spain: Editorial Espasa Calpe, S. A.; 2001).

21 See Bergen, "A Simplified Approach for Teaching the Gender of Spanish Nouns," p. 873. In Mexico, for example, most speakers would not know these ambiforms. There's a town in California called "La Puente," left over from these earlier days.

22 The first known recorded use of the Spanish *embarazar* seems to be in 1460 in *Cancionero de Stúñiga* (Songbook of Stúñiga). However in 1460 the word *embarazar* does not refer to pregnancy, whose common terminology was *preñada*, still at that date. By the publication of the 1732 *DRAE*, *embarazada* appears as "adj. La mujer que está preñada. Gravida, pregnans." For a discussion of pregnancy and embarrassment, see Gail Kern Paster, *The Body Embarrassed: Drama and the Disciplines of Shame in Early Modern England* (Ithica, NY Cornell University Press, 1993).

23 They, also, argued "*nacimiento* (defined in the *DRAE* as '*acción y efecto de nacer*') is masculine in Spanish because it is related to the '*el efecto*' than to the '*la acción*' in the same way that '*nascimento*' in Italian was masculine (a term more used in literature, which was replaced for the more common *nascita*, feminine)." But then in Spanish, they pointed out, there is also *natividad*, feminine, which means the same as *nacimiento*. It is used less in common language than in religion, the "Natividad de Jesucristo." Their position, therefore, is purely phonological. "In sum, most of these words are masculine," they say, "and masculine in all three languages, because they derive from masculine Latin words. When you find one of them that is feminine, you can find it in the feminine in the other languages as well (such as *la grossese, la graviditá, la gravidez*, or *naissance/nascita/natividad*)."

24 According to the *DRAE*, *embarazo* means "1. impedimento, dificultad, obstáculo 2. Estado en que se halla la hembra gestante 3. Encogimiento, falta de soltura en los modales o en la acción" and derives from *baraza*. The *Arabic English Dictionary of Modern Written Arabic* defines *baraza* as "something that is protruding, prominent, or raised." The Spanish word might come from the Portuguese version of the Arabic *baraza*, *embaraçar*, as well, which might be a combination of the prefix *em-* (from Latin *in-* for in-) with *baraça* (a noose or rope), which accords with the synonym *encinta* (on noose, on rope), referring to the old custom in which women wore a strap of cloth on their dresses when pregnant. (Hans Wehr and J. Milton Cowan, *Arabic English Dictionary of Modern Written Arabic*, 4th ed. [Urbana, IL: Spoken Language Services, 1993]).

25 See Everett for another discussion of grammar and culture. Dan Everett, "Cultural Constraints on Grammar and Cognition in Pirahã: Another look at the design features of human language," *Current Anthropology* 46 (4): 621–646.

26 Collier, *From Duty to Desire*, pp. 3–113, and "From Mary to Modern Woman: The material basis of Marianismo and its transformation in a Spanish village," *American Ethnologist* 13, no. 1 (February 1985): 100–107.

27 In Italian: *il sesso* (sex, masculine), *l'amore* (love, masculine), *il matrimonio* (marriage, masculine), *la gravidanza* (pregnancy, feminine), *il parto* (childbirth, the actual event, masculine), *la nascita* (birth, feminine). In French: *le sexe* (sex, masculine), *l'amour* (love, masculine, was feminine in the Middle Ages), *le marriage* (marriage, masculine), *la grossesse* (pregnancy, feminine), *l'accouchement* or *l'enfantement* (childbirth, the actual event, masculine), *la naissance* (birth, feminine).

28 For more on connecting paternity, paternalism, and padres in Spain, see Collier, *From Duty to Desire*, pp. 153–176; and Julio Casares, *Diccionario ideológico de la lengua española: desde la idea a la palabra, desde la palabra a la idea*, 2nd ed. (Barcelona, Spain: Gustavo Gili, 1997).

SOUNDING IT OUT

1 My emphasis. Pierre J. Bancel, Alain Matthey de l'Etang, and Merritt Ruhlen, "Language in the Cradle (2): The proto-human words

PAPA and MAMA and the origin of articulate language," paper presented at the Cradle of Language Conference, Stellenbosch, South Africa, November 6–10, 2006, p. 2; Pierre J. Bancel and Alain Matthey de l'Etang, "Tracing the Ancestral Kinship System: The Global Etymon KAKA, Part I: A linguistic study," *Mother Tongue* 7 (2002): 209–244, and "Tracing the Ancestral Kinship System: The Global Etymon KAKA, Part II: An anthropological study," *Mother Tongue* 7 (2002): 245–258.

2 Alain Matthey de l'Etang and Pierre J. Bancel, "The Age of Mama and Papa," in *Hot Pursuit of Language in Prehistory: Essays in the four fields of anthropology*, ed. John D. Bengtson (Amsterdam, Netherlands: John Benjamins Publishing Co., 2008), p. 417.

3 Bancel and Matthey de l'Etang, "Language in the Cradle," p. 1.

4 Roman Jakobson, "Why 'mama' and 'papa'?" in *Selected Writings, Vol. I: Phonological Studies* (The Hague: Mouton, 1962), pp. 538–545.

5 G. P. Murdock, "World Ethnographic Sample," *American Anthropologist* 59 (1957): 664–687, and "Cross-Language Parallels in Parental Kin Terms," *Anthropological Linguistics* 1, no. 9 (1959): 1–5.

6 Michelle Bigenho notes that in Bolivia the verb mamar also appears in expressions, such as one she heard her colleagues say, "Después de 502 años los españoles nos siguen mamando." Bigenho attempts a translation this way: "'After 502 years they (the Spaniards) keep tricking us' or 'keep pulling the wool over our eyes' 'keep sucking us dry' or 'keep taking us in.'" She explains that "the literal meaning paints a picture that should not be ignored. To receive nourishment a baby nurses at its mother's breast. Past a certain age, the baby does not need the mother's milk, but may resist weaning. Deception is rooted behind the expression 'está mamando.' . . . The mother may give in and let her child nurse, but she knows that she has been coaxed into letting the child have his or her way." *Sounding Indigenous: Authenticity in Bolivian music performance* (New York: Palgrave Macmillan, 2002), p. 82.

7 William Tecumseh Sherman Fitch III, "Vocal Tract Length Perception and the Evolution of Language," Unpublished dissertation, Brown University, Providence, Rhode Island, 1986.

8 Plato. *Cratylus*, trans. B. Jowett (Whitefish, MT: Kessinger Publishing, 2004), p. 21.

9 Ibid., p. 94.

10 The *DRAE*. Also see Mark Pagel, Quentin D. Atkinson, and Andrew Meade, "Frequency of Word-Use Predicts Rates of Lexical Evolution Throughout Indo-European History," *Nature* 449 (October 2007): 717–720.

10 W. F. Leopold, *Speech Development of a Bilingual Child, 1: Vocabulary growth in the first two years* (Evanston & Chicago, IL: Northwestern University, 1939), and *Speech Development of a Bilingual Child, 2: Sound learning in the first two years* (Evanston, IL: Northwestern University, 1947).

12 Alice Kaplan, in her book on the French language, said it best: "He [Jacques Lacan] believed that the child gains access to language only when it perceives the existence of the father . . . But it is mothers, traditionally, who teach language, who listen and correct, it is mothers who are the first to hear new words. It is mothers who break or heal a child's tongue" (Alice Kaplan, *French Lessons: A memoir* [Chicago, IL: University of Chicago Press, 1993], p. 99).

13 *Diccionario de Uso del Español*, 2nd ed., ed. María Moliner (Madrid, Spain: Editorial Gredos, S. A., 1998), p. 627.

BACK TO CHURCH

1 For a historical explanation of kissing in parks in Mexico, see William H. Beezley and Professor Colin M. Maclaughlin, PhD, *Mexicans in Revolution, 1910–1946* (Lincoln: University of Nebraska Press, 2009), pp. 47–79.

2 Thomas V. Gamkrelidze and V. V. Ivanov, "The Early History of Indo-European Languages," *Scientific American* (March 1990): 110. Also Colin Renfrew, *Archaeology and Language: The puzzle of the Indo-European origins* (Cambridge, UK: Cambridge University Press, 1988).

3 For the history of Spanish, other than dictionaries and literature, I drew upon the following sources: Ralph Penny, *A History of the Spanish Language*, 2nd ed. (Cambridge, UK: Cambridge University Press (2002); David A. Pharies, *A Brief History of the Spanish Language* (Chicago, IL: University of Chicago Press, 2007).

4 *DRAE*, 2001.

5 *Madrigal's* derivation from *mater* seems clear. However, there are sources that associate it with the Latin root *maturicare* and *maturus*: "Madrigal, Sp. Fr. Madrigal, It. Madrigale, madriale, originally mandriale, a pastoral song, from Latin and Greek mandra, a sheep-fold. The word was perhaps mentally connected with madrugar (Sp. and Portg.), to rise (L. Lat. maturicare from maturus), to rise early, as if a 'morning-song,' like aube and aubades, and serenade 'evening song,' from sera. The Italian word has also been analyzed into madre gala, 'song of the Virgin' . . . but incorrectly" (Rev. A. Smythe Palmer, *Folk-Etymology: A dictionary of verbal corruptions or words perverted in form or meaning by false derivation or mistaken analogy* [London: George Bell and Sons, 1882]). In contemporary sources, more commonly one finds entries such as this one: "Italian madrigale, probably from dialectal madregal, simple, from Late Latin mātrīcālis, invented, original, from Latin, of the womb, from mātrīx, mātrīa, womb, from māter, mātr-, mother; see mater" (*The American Heritage Dictionary of the English Language*, 4th ed. [Boston, MA: Houghton Mifflin Company, 2009]). Or madrigal, a "'short love poem,' also 'part-song for three or more voices,' 1588, from It. (Venetian) *madregal*, 'simple, ingenuous,' from L.L. *matricalis*, 'invented, original,' lit. 'of or from the womb,' from *matrix* (gen. *matricis*) 'womb'" (Douglas Harper, *Online Etymology Dictionary*, retrieved November 5, 2009).

6 Sources drawn upon for this section, along with those cited, include David W. Anthony, "Migration in Archaeology: The baby and the bathwater," *American Anthropologist* 92, no. 4 (December 1990): 895–914; Peter Boyd-Bowman, *From Latin to Romance in Sound Charts* (Washington, DC: Georgetown University, 1980 [1954]); Robbins Burling, "Review: On the origin of languages: Studies in linguistic taxonomy," *The Journal of the Royal Anthropological Institute* 1, no. 4 (December 1995): 857–858; Andrew Carstairs-McCarthy, "The Origin of Language: Tracing the origin of mother tongue," *Language* 73, no. 3 (September 1997): 611–614; Joseph H. Greenberg, "Review: Archaeology and Language: The puzzle of Indo-European origins," *American Anthropologist* 90, no. 4 (December, 1988): 1029–1030; József Herman, *Vulgar Latin* (Park, PA: Pennsylvania State University Press, 2000 [1967]); Penny, *A History of the Spanish Language*; Pharies, *A Brief History of the Spanish Language*; Rebecca Posner, *The Romance Languages* (New York: Cambridge University Press, 1996); Renfrew, *Archaeology and Language*.

7 Islam was not banned in the kingdoms of Aragon until 1525–1526,

after Charles V became emperor, and the formal expulsion of most of the Moriscos did not occur until 1609–1614. Islam was originally left legal in Granada in the surrender accords of 1492.

8 Division of labor existed before that, of course, with men on occasion hunting and women daily gathering nuts and fruits, hunting small game, and caring for the old and young. Rituals existed, as well, especially when the men returned from their hunt and the large carcasses were divided up and handed out to villagers.

9 Robert Bartlett, *The Making of Europe*: *Conquest, colonization, and cultural change, 950–1350* (Princeton, NJ: Princeton University Press, 1994).

10 Claudio Lomnitz, who focused not on the symbolic, somatic, or gendered aspects of Spanish, but the fact of it, noted, "The Spanish language in the Indies was not simply an arbitrary tongue among others, it was the suitable language in which to communicate the mysteries of the Catholic faith. Even today in Mexico, *hablar en cristiano* ("to speak in Christian") is synonymous with speaking in Spanish." Claudio Lomnitz, *Deep Mexico Silent Mexico: An anthropology of nationalism* (Minneapolis: University of Minnesota Press, 2001), pp. 1-34. While Lomnitz notes that Spanish was seen by those in Spain, including Carlos V, as a modern form of Latin, and, therefore, most appropriate for communicating the faith, there is irony in this. The Latin from which Spanish evolved was not the ecclesiastical, written Latin of the Holy Catholic Church, which persisted well into the twentieth century, but the spoken vernacular of the Roman soldier.

11 Gregory R. Crane, ed., *Perseus Digital Library Project*, http://www .perseus.tufts.edu/; University of Notre Dame Latin Dictionary and Grammar Aid, http://www.archives.nd.edu; *DRAE*, 2002. Here vota, neuter plural, became feminine due to phonological reasons, vota, plural, the vows of bride and groom (Pharies, *A Brief History of the Spanish Language*, p. 105).

12 "La mujer, cuyas principales dotes son la abnegación, la belleza, la compasión, la perspicacia y la ternura debe dar y dará al marido obediencia, agrado, asistencia, consuelo y consejo, tratándolo siempre con la veneración que se debe a la persona que nos apoya y defiende, y con la delicadeza de quien no quiere exasperar la parte brusca, irritable y dura de sí mismo propia de su carácter. El uno y el otro se deben y tendrán

respeto, deferencia, fidelidad, confianza y ternura, ambos procurarán que lo que el uno se esperaba del otro al unirse con él, no vaya a desmentirse con la unión" (The woman, whose main attributes are self-abnegation, beauty, compassion, shrewdness and tenderness, must give and shall always give her husband obedience, affability, attention, comfort and advice, treating him with the reverence due to the person who supports and defends us and with the delicacy of someone who wishes not to exasperate the brusque, irritable and harsh components of his character. One and the other should and does act with respect, deference, loyalty, trust and tenderness, understanding that both desire to accord with him, to not contradict the union.) Melchor Ocampo, "Epístola," in *Ley del Matrimonio Civil, Legislación mexicana: ó, colección completa de las disposiciones legislativas expedidas desde la independencia de la república*, eds. Manuel Dublán and José María Lozano (México: Imprenta del Comercio, a cargo de Dublán y Lozano, Hijos, 1876–1912), Vol. 8, Disposition 4604–5135, 1856–1860, 23 julio de 1859, pp. 691–694; Justo Sierra, quoted in Mary K. Vaughn, "Women, Class and Education in Mexico 1880–1928," in *Women in Latin America*, ed. W. Bollinger et al. (Riverside, CA: Latin American Perspectives, 1979), pp. 63–80.

13 C. M. Stafford Poole, *Our Lady of Guadalupe: The origins and sources of a Mexican national symbol, 1531–1797* (Tucson, AZ: University of Arizona Press, 1995), and *The Guadalupan Controversies in Mexico* (Stanford, CA: Stanford University Press, 2006).

14 The precise date or dates for the Ave Maria as established prayer is unknown. The *Catholic Encyclopedia* documents its use as early as the eleventh century (Herbert Thurston, *Catholic Encyclopedia: An international work of reference on the constitution, doctrine, discipline, and history of the Catholic church*, vol. 7, ed. Charles G. Herbermann, Edward A. Pace, Condé B. Pallen, Thomas J. Shahan, John J. Wynne; assisted by numerous collaborators [New York: Robert Appleton Company, 1907–1912], pp. 110–112). However, it is possible that it was used in prayer as early as the seventh century. What is remarkable is how little the prayer has changed over the centuries, outside the variations that translations create. The names Mary and Jesus, which did not appear in the original lines found in Luke (1:28,42), were added so that by the thirteenth century the Ave Maria was "Hail Mary, full of grace, the Lord Jesus is with thee. Blessed art thou amongst women and blessed is the fruit of thy womb." Then sometime before 1495 a second change occurred, which was the

petition "Holy Mary, Mother of God, pray for us sinners, now and in the hour of our death. Amen" and which the authors of the Council of Trent included in 1556 in the *Catechisms* of 1556. According to one source, the petition first appeared in print in 1495 in Girolamo Savonarola's *Esposizione sopra l'Ave Maria*. The Hail Mary prayer in Savonarola's exposition reads: "Ave Maria gratia plena Dominus tecum Benedicta tu in mulieribus et benedictus Fructus uentris tui Iesus sancta Maria mater Dei ora pro nobis peccatoribus nunc et in hora mortis. Amen" (Hail Mary, full of grace, the Lord is with thee; blessed art thou among women, and blessed is the fruit of thy womb, Jesus. Holy Mary, Mother of God, pray for us sinners, now and at the hour of our death. Amen). Girolamo Savonarola, *Esposizione Sopra l'Ave Maria* (Florence, Italy: Bartolommeo di Libri, 1495). British Library, Rare Books Department, Shelfmark: IA 27542.

15. Jaroslav Pelikan, *Mary Through the Centuries* (New Haven, CT: Yale University Press, 1996), p. 14.

16 Before the first session of Trent began in 1545 the native populations in Mexico were already expected to know the Ave Maria. It is argued by some that in both Catholic England and Spain in the sixteenth century there is a major move to Christ-focused worship. See William A. Christian Jr., *Local Religion in Sixteenth Century Spain* (Princeton, NJ: Princeton University Press, 1981); Eamon Duffy, *The Stripping of the Altars: Traditional religion in England, c. 1400–c. 1580* (New Haven, CT: Yale University Press, 1993). Nevertheless, in Mexico the Dominicans, at least, were very interested in the Rosary and Mary. See Byron Hamann, "Bad Christians, New Spains: Catholics, Muslims, and Native Americans in a transatlantic world," Unpublished dissertation, University of Chicago, forthcoming 2010.

17 This was pointed out by Beauvoir back in the 1950s and then picked up by other scholars. See Simone de Beauvoir, *The Second Sex* (New York: Alfred A. Knopf, Inc., 1952); Mary Daly, *The Church and the Second Sex* (Boston, MA: Beacon Press, 1985); Nancy Jay, *Throughout Your Generations Forever: Sacrifice, religion and paternity* (Chicago, IL: University of Chicago Press, 1992); Gerda Lerner, *The Creation of Patriarchy* (New York: Oxford University Press, Inc., 1986).

18 Pelikan, *Mary Through the Centuries*, p. 16.

19 Ibid., p. 20.

20 The Council of Trent, *The Canons and Decrees of the Sacred and Oecumenical Council of Trent, The Twenty-fourth Session*, ed. and trans. by J. Waterworth (London: Dolman, 1848), pp. 192–232.

21 Bartlett, *The Making of Europe*.

22 "Madre," the *DRAE* in 2009 defines, is "hembra quien ha parido" (a female who has given birth). It does not say a woman who has given birth. But for *"padre,"* it defines *varón* and *macho* on the same line: "que ha engendrado" (a man or male who has sired children, emphasizing the sociology *and* biology of the male contribution). *DRAE*, 2001.

23 *The American Heritage Dictionary of the English Language*, 4th ed.; *The Oxford Spanish Dictionary*, ed. B. G. Jarman, R. Russell, C. Carvajal, and J. Horwood (New York: Oxford University Press, Inc., 2001); *DRAE*, 1970, 1984, 2001. *Webster's Revised Unabridged Dictionary* (Plainfield, NJ: MICRA, Inc., 1996, 1998); *WordNet* 2.0. Princeton University, 2003.

MADRE

1 This chapter benefited from conversations and correspondence with William H. Beezley (University of Arizona), William T. French (University of British Columbia), and (via the former) Carmen Nava (UAM–Xochimilco, Mexico City) between July 2008 and January 2010. In addition, it draws upon the following sources: William H. Beezley and Colin M. MacLachlan, *The Essential Mexico* (New York: Oxford University Press, forthcoming) for a discussion of the *Epistle* as the essential statement of gender relations and marriage in Mexico for the last century and a half; William E. French, "Cartas, cuerpos y crímenes: Rapto y estupro en el Chichuahua porfiriano y revolucionario," paper given in a session entitled "Amor y crimen: Experiencia, leyes y justicia, últimas décadas del siglo XIX y primeras de XX" (XIII Reunión de Historidores de México, Estados Unidos y Canada, held in Querétaro, México, October 26-30, 2010) for a discussion of love letters, the law, and marital relations at the turn of the nineteenth century; Benito Pablo Juárez García, *Apuntes para mis hijos*, Ilustraciones de Alberto Beltran (Mexico, D.F.: Comisión Nacional para la Conmemoración del Centenario del Fallecimiento de Don Benito Juárez, 1972); Angeles Mendieta Alatorre, *Margarita Maza de Juárez: Epistolario, antología, iconografía y efemérides* (Mexico, D.F.: Comisión Nacional para la Conmemoración del Centenario del Fallecimiento de Don Benito Juárez, 1972); Jorge L.

Tamayo, *Epistolario de Benito Juárez*, 2nd ed. (Mexico, D.F.: Fondo de Cultura Económica, 1972).

2 See "Back to Church," footnote 12.

3 Oaxaca is in the process of writing a new epistle, however. In fall 2009, the state government asked for submissions from residents, and it is offering a 30,000 peso reward (approximately $3,000) for the best one.

4 Justo Sierra quoted in Mary K. Vaughn, "Women, Class and Education in Mexico 1880–1928," in *Women in Latin America,* ed. W. Bollinger et al. (Riverside, CA: Latin American Perspectives, 1979), pp. 63–80.

5 Liza Bakewell, "*Bella Artes* and *Artes Populares:* the implications of difference," in *Looking High and Low: Art and cultural identity*, ed. Brenda Bright and Liza Bakewell (Tucson: University of Arizona Press, 1995).

6 Arrom, *The Women of Mexico City, 1790–1857*, p. 253.

7 In a carefully nuanced discussion of Mexican nationalism, which included the "nationalization of the church," Claudio Lomnitz argues that for Mexico the nation "emerges as an offshoot of religious expansionism" (rather than as a secular enterprise generally associated with nation building), which began with Columbus and continued right through independence from Spain and up to the modern era. Lomnitz, *Deep Mexico Silent Mexico*, p. 21. On another note, I'm often asked about pre-Columbian influences. In the pre-Columbian pantheon, goddesses, who were also mothers, had complicated reputations, often as life-giving as they were life-taking. I never saw any evidence, however, for an influence of these goddesses on the madres of this book. See Blanca Solares, *Madre Terrible: La Diosa en la religión del México antiguo* (México: Anthropos Editorial, 2007).

8 The other reason is that the State owns all Catholic churches in Mexico, as stated in Article 27 of the 1917 Constitution. Salinas, when changing Articles of the Constitution to accommodate Church requests for reappropriation of their power and property, held on to that part of the Article. They are curated by the Secretary of Public Education's offices.

9 Juan Carlos Zavala, "Oaxaqueños malinchistas, no aceptan productors de casa," *Desperatar de Oaxaca*, February 22, 2009, p. 13.

ACKNOWLEDGMENTS

SPECIAL THANKS TO my friends and acquaintances who appear, one way or another, in this book: Monica Anaya de Alba, Laura Anderson Barbata, Pablo Arredondo Ramírez, Avery Oakleaf Bakewell, Jennie Woodhouse Bakewell, Karen Ballesteros, William H. Beezley, Amparo Bonilla, Sarah Boyce Borzilleri, Stanley Brandes, Tony Brodziak, Amapola (Poppy) Burke, Jane Bussey, Lilian Carrillo, Teresa Cito, Elena Climent, Christiane Corbat, Liliana Dones Villegas, Moisés Espinosa, Tecumseh W. S. Fitch III, Gloria Garcia, Luis Garduño, José Alejandro González Gómez, Delia M. Greth, Byron Ellsworth Hamann, Laura Hernández, John Landry, Magali Lara, Odette León Martinez, Zeferina Judith Murguía, Davíd Montaña, Albertano Nolasco Cruz, Juliana Parra Boutot, Adrienne Pine, Jesusa Rodríguez, Rochelle Rosen, Claudia Schatán, Raquel Tibol, Aurora Torres Varela, María Aurea Toxqui, Celia Vargas, Santiago Villegas, and Enrique Yepes.

Many thanks to all my other friends, acquaintances, colleagues, and venues whose gifts to the book come from their contributions to my thinking in general; their senses of humor; their insights on life, language, mothers, fathers, children, politics, history, Spanish, English, all Romance languages, Latin America, Mexico, the United States: José (Pepe) Amor y Vásquez, Arabica

Café in Portland (Maine), Lynda Barry's Writing the Unthinkable Workshop, Charles Beatty Medina, William O. Beeman, Kathy Biberstein, Michelle Bigenho, Carrie Chorba, Ian Corbin, April Covington, Los Cuiles Café in Oaxaca, Katherine Demuth, Carlos Fuentes, Frederick Fullerton, William E. French, Richard B. Gann, the late Irving Goldman, Celeste Gonzalez de Bustamante, James Green, Maria Elena Gomez Sanchez, Linda Henderson, Susan Hirsch, Kaia Huseby, Lyman Johnson, Jon Kabat-Zinn, Lily King, Louise Lamphere, Bayard Love, Julia Majors, Andrew S. Matthews, Anne Mayagoitia, Kerry Michaels, Mary Moran, Kenneth Case Newman, Lucile Newman, Sharon Olds and her New Poems Workshop, Antonio Ortega, Luisa Puig, Marcia Quiñones, Monica Rankin, Susan Reed, John Phillip Santos, Dalines Senteño, Laura Sewall, Thomas Skidmore, Summer Solstice Writing Group, Zak Stone, Alan Symonds, Patricia Symonds, Jane Szurek, Barbara Tedlock, Sirpa Tenhunen, Abigail Thomas and her Memoir Workshop, Heli Uusikyla, Jake Wien, Nathaniel Wolfson, and Sherman Wilcox.

Special thanks to the Fulbright-García Robles Program, the National Science Foundation, Rocky Mountain Council on Latin American Studies, Colgate University, Thomas J. Watson Jr. Institute for International Studies, and Center for Latin American and Caribbean Studies at Brown University for support, platforms, and/or offices.

Many thanks to my first full-draft readers for their critical comments: Byron Ellsworth Hamann, Luis Iturbe, Claudia Schatán, Lindsay Sterling, and Francisco Valdés Ugalde. And finally, many thanks to my agent Anne Depue and my editor Alane Salierno Mason, vice president and senior editor at W. W. Norton, and her editorial assistant, Denise Scarfi, for their wise edits.

Last, because most of all, many thanks to my family, all nineteen of them.

INDEX

ABOUT THE AUTHOR

Liza Bakewell is a writer and anthropologist who lives with her two daughters on the coast of Maine. She holds a doctorate in anthropology; she has taught courses in language, art, and gender at Brown University, Bowdoin College, and Colgate University; and she currently directs The Mesolore Project at the Center for Latin American and Caribbean Studies at Brown. Her writing has appeared in *Words without Borders: The online magazine for international literature, Humanistic Quarterly, Frontiers: A journal of women's studies, American Anthropologist*, the *Encyclopedia of Mexico, Mesolore: The cybercenter for research and teaching on Mesoamerica*, and other publications.